OPPOSING
VIEWPOINTS®
SERIES

The Prison Industrial Complex

Other Books of Related Interest

Opposing Viewpoints Series
Immigration Bans
Mandatory Minimum Sentences
Mass Incarceration

At Issue Series
The Death Penalty
Guns: Conceal and Carry
Wrongful Conviction and Exoneration

Current Controversies Series
America's Mental Health Crisis
Deporting Immigrants
Learned Helplessness, Welfare, and the Poverty Cycle

> "Congress shall make no law … abridging the freedom of speech, or of the press."

First Amendment to the US Constitution

The basic foundation of our democracy is the First Amendment guarantee of freedom of expression. The Opposing Viewpoints series is dedicated to the concept of this basic freedom and the idea that it is more important to practice it than to enshrine it.

OPPOSING
VIEWPOINTS®
SERIES

The Prison Industrial Complex

Lita Sorensen, Book Editor

GREENHAVEN
PUBLISHING

Published in 2021 by Greenhaven Publishing, LLC
353 3rd Avenue, Suite 255, New York, NY 10010

Copyright © 2021 by Greenhaven Publishing, LLC

First Edition

Articles in Greenhaven Publishing anthologies are often edited for length to meet page
requirements. In addition, original titles of these works are changed to clearly present
the main thesis and to explicitly indicate the author's opinion. Every effort is made to
ensure that Greenhaven Publishing accurately reflects the original intent of the authors.
Every effort has been made to trace the owners of the copyrighted material.

Cover image: Ann Johansson/Getty Images

Library of Congress Cataloging-in-Publication Data

Names: Sorensen, Lita, editor.
Title: The prison industrial complex / Lita Sorensen, book editor.
Description: First edition. | New York, NY : Greenhaven Publishing, 2021. |
    Series: Opposing viewpoints | Includes bibliographical references and
    index. | Audience: Grades 9–12.
Identifiers: LCCN 2020003149 | ISBN 9781534506916 (library binding) | ISBN
    9781534506909 (paperback)
Subjects: LCSH: Prison-industrial complex—United States—Juvenile
    literature.
Classification: LCC HV9471 .P746 2021 | DDC 365/.973—dc23
LC record available at https://lccn.loc.gov/2020003149

Manufactured in the United States of America

Website: http://greenhavenpublishing.com

Contents

Chapter 1: What Is the Prison Industrial Complex?

Chapter 2: How Did We Get Here?

The Importance of Opposing Viewpoints

P erhaps every generation experiences a period in time in which the populace seems especially polarized, starkly divided on the important issues of the day and gravitating toward the far ends of the political spectrum and away from a consensus-facilitating middle ground. The world that today's students are growing up in and that they will soon enter into as active and engaged citizens is deeply fragmented in just this way. Issues relating to terrorism, immigration, women's rights, minority rights, race relations, health care, taxation, wealth and poverty, the environment, policing, military intervention, the proper role of government—in some ways, perennial issues that are freshly and uniquely urgent and vital with each new generation—are currently roiling the world.

If we are to foster a knowledgeable, responsible, active, and engaged citizenry among today's youth, we must provide them with the intellectual, interpretive, and critical-thinking tools and experience necessary to make sense of the world around them and of the all-important debates and arguments that inform it. After all, the outcome of these debates will in large measure determine the future course, prospects, and outcomes of the world and its peoples, particularly its youth. If they are to become successful members of society and productive and informed citizens, students need to learn how to evaluate the strengths and weaknesses of someone else's arguments, how to sift fact from opinion and fallacy, and how to test the relative merits and validity of their own opinions against the known facts and the best possible available information. The landmark series Opposing Viewpoints has been providing students with just such critical-thinking skills and exposure to the debates surrounding society's most urgent contemporary issues for many years, and it continues to serve this essential role with undiminished commitment, care, and rigor.

The key to the series's success in achieving its goal of sharpening students' critical-thinking and analytic skills resides in its title—

Opposing Viewpoints. In every intriguing, compelling, and engaging volume of this series, readers are presented with the widest possible spectrum of distinct viewpoints, expert opinions, and informed argumentation and commentary, supplied by some of today's leading academics, thinkers, analysts, politicians, policy makers, economists, activists, change agents, and advocates. Every opinion and argument anthologized here is presented objectively and accorded respect. There is no editorializing in any introductory text or in the arrangement and order of the pieces. No piece is included as a "straw man," an easy ideological target for cheap point-scoring. As wide and inclusive a range of viewpoints as possible is offered, with no privileging of one particular political ideology or cultural perspective over another. It is left to each individual reader to evaluate the relative merits of each argument—as he or she sees it, and with the use of ever-growing critical-thinking skills—and grapple with his or her own assumptions, beliefs, and perspectives to determine how convincing or successful any given argument is and how the reader's own stance on the issue may be modified or altered in response to it.

This process is facilitated and supported by volume, chapter, and selection introductions that provide readers with the essential context they need to begin engaging with the spotlighted issues, with the debates surrounding them, and with their own perhaps shifting or nascent opinions on them. In addition, guided reading and discussion questions encourage readers to determine the authors' point of view and purpose, interrogate and analyze the various arguments and their rhetoric and structure, evaluate the arguments' strengths and weaknesses, test their claims against available facts and evidence, judge the validity of the reasoning, and bring into clearer, sharper focus the reader's own beliefs and conclusions and how they may differ from or align with those in the collection or those of their classmates.

Research has shown that reading comprehension skills improve dramatically when students are provided with compelling, intriguing, and relevant "discussable" texts. The subject matter of these collections could not be more compelling, intriguing, or urgently relevant to today's students and the world they are poised to inherit. The anthologized articles and the reading and discussion questions that are included with them also provide the basis for stimulating, lively, and passionate classroom debates. Students who are compelled to anticipate objections to their own argument and identify the flaws in those of an opponent read more carefully, think more critically, and steep themselves in relevant context, facts, and information more thoroughly. In short, using discussable text of the kind provided by every single volume in the Opposing Viewpoints series encourages close reading, facilitates reading comprehension, fosters research, strengthens critical thinking, and greatly enlivens and energizes classroom discussion and participation. The entire learning process is deepened, extended, and strengthened.

For all of these reasons, Opposing Viewpoints continues to be exactly the right resource at exactly the right time—when we most need to provide readers with the critical-thinking tools and skills that will not only serve them well in school but also in their careers and their daily lives as decision-making family members, community members, and citizens. This series encourages respectful engagement with and analysis of opposing viewpoints and fosters a resulting increase in the strength and rigor of one's own opinions and stances. As such, it helps make readers "future ready," and that readiness will pay rich dividends for the readers themselves, for the citizenry, for our society, and for the world at large.

Introduction

> *"The prison industrial complex is not only a set of interest groups and institutions. It is also a state of mind. The lure of big money is corrupting the nation's criminal justice system, replacing notions of public service with a drive for higher profits."*
>
> —Eric Schlosser, "The Prison-Industrial Complex," The Atlantic

The United States is a nation on lockdown—literally. A frequently quoted statistic holds that as a nation, the United States contains only 5 percent of the world's population, but 25 percent of the world's prisons. To many of us living in the United States, encountering that statistic for the first time can be a complete shock.

Perhaps equally as shocking is the very real possibility that the shirt you're wearing, purchased at the Target down the road, may have been sewn by an inmate. Or that the Starbucks you visit after school originally became everyone's favorite coffee by using cheap prison labor in the early 2000s to exponentially grow the brand so other coffee shops couldn't compete.

So, what exactly is the prison industrial complex, or PIC, as it is known by acronym? As Eric Schlosser notes above, it is a collection of private prisons, interest groups, and institutions. But it is also a mindset. The idea of retribution vs. rehabilitation inherent in the criminal justice system is an old one, dating back as far as the Code of Hammurabi (created circa 1754 BCE), allowing for the idea of severe punishment and vengeance meted out to those who commit crimes.

Currently, the prison industrial complex and all that it includes—from private prison corporations specializing in handling immigrant detention, to companies that provide things such as food service to prisons, to large national corporations contracting prison labor to sell their brand—is on the rise in America. This was especially true under the Trump administration, although the prison industrial complex got its start long before Donald Trump became president.

Opposing Viewpoints: The Prison Industrial Complex seeks to introduce the reader to a variety of perspectives and viewpoints surrounding the prison industrial complex as a social construct and in a greater sense, as an overall state of mind. In chapters titled "What Is the Prison Industrial Complex?" "How Did We Get Here?" "What Are the Economic and Social Implications of the Prison Industrial Complex?" and What Is the Future of the Prison Industrial Complex?" viewpoint authors explore the laws and policies that resulted in mass incarceration and the private prisons that benefit financially from the incarcerated. They examine the segments of the population—usually the most vulnerable, such as women, the mentally ill, people of color, immigrants, and teens—that are affected by the prison industrial complex, often indelibly. And they look to the future, to prison reform and solutions for breaking out of the system that is now so enmeshed in society.

CHAPTER 1

What Is the Prison Industrial Complex?

Chapter Preface

The number of people currently incarcerated in prisons in the United States has risen by 700 percent in the last 40 years. One might think this massive increase was precipitated by a rise in the violent crime rate, but that is not the case.

The actual reasons behind such an increase in the prison population manifest what is collectively known as the prison industrial complex, and it is largely a US phenomenon. They include harsh sentencing laws and other crime legislation that increases prison populations, the exploitation of cheap labor, the lack of resources to treat social problems at their root, and simple greed and the desire to turn a profit.

The viewpoints in this chapter provide an overview of the prison industrial complex (PIC) to those who may not be familiar with what it entails. In short, it is a collection of private industries, laws, and lobbyist groups that profit or have interest in the establishment and continuance of a prison-based economy.

From a variety of perspectives, viewpoint authors offer examinations of the largest companies profiting from the prison industrial complex. They also introduce the reader to the concept of institutional racism and how racial injustice is propagated in various ways through a system of laws and stereotypes, creating mass social inequality.

> *"As of 2009, 7,225,800 people were
> under some form of correctional
> supervision (jail, prison, or
> parole), about 3.1% of the entire
> US population at the time. At the
> moment more than 1 in 99 people
> are imprisoned."*

What Is the Prison Industrial Complex?
Ozy Frantz

*In the following viewpoint, Ozy Frantz examines the prison industrial
complex as a uniquely US phenomenon. The author notes that the
rise of the prison industrial complex can be traced directly to the
War on Drugs and harsher sentencing laws. The cycle is vicious,
he writes, as there is a lot of money to be made from the system,
and incarceration serves to perpetuate the cycle rather than offering
rehabilitation. Ozy Frantz wrote this for the Good Men Project, an
organization founded as a way for men to tell personal stories about
what it means to be "a good man" in today's society.*

"What Is the Prison-Industrial Complex?," by Ozy Frantz, Good Men Project.com, August
14, 2012. Previously published on the Good Men project. Used with permission.

As you read, consider the following questions:

1. What are the three reasons the author gives for the explosion of the United States prison population?
2. Why do you think looking at the prison industrial complex through a country-specific lens is important?
3. Why might an organization like the Good Men Project find this topic important to its focus?

P rison-industrial complex" is one of those terms like "rape culture" that refers to less a single identifiable thing and more a giant mess of cultural attitudes, beliefs, institutions, structures, and perverse incentives. It can be briefly summed up as "the interdependent economic and social interests that contribute to America's extraordinarily high rate of incarceration."

The prison-industrial complex in the form I'm discussing is primarily a USA phenomenon; while of course elements of it exist in other countries, the US has been the most assiduous about putting the prison-industrial complex into practice. America has the single highest reported rate of incarceration in the world, although admittedly some countries like North Korea blatantly lie and may have higher incarceration rates than America. Seriously, good job America, we're possibly behind the single most totalitarian government in the world!

As of 2009, 7,225,800 people were under some form of correctional supervision (jail, prison, or parole), about 3.1% of the entire US population at the time. At the moment more than 1 in 99 people are imprisoned. Since 1970, the number of people in prison has increased 700%. Respected groups that oppose the high level of incarceration in the US include Human Rights Watch and the American Civil Liberties Union. There is a problem here, Americans!

What Caused the Rise of the Prison-Industrial Complex?

The number of people in prison has increased 700% since 1970. Is it just because people are committing more violent crimes now? Actually, no, the rate of violent crimes has been decreasing for two decades, while the number of people in prison rises. (In case you're thinking that the imprisonment caused the drop in crime—nope, Canada experienced a lower crime rate as well, despite not putting three percent of its population under correctional supervision.) In addition, approximately 52.4% of prisoners in state prisons and 7.9% in federal prisons are in for violent crimes, which means that the majority of the prisoners in the United States are not in prison for violent crimes.

The first answer is the drug war. The number of people in prison for drug offenses rose twelvefold from 1980 to 2003. In 2010 1,638,846 people in the US were arrested for nonviolent drug charges. Starting in 1973 with the formation of the Drug Enforcement Administration and reaching its peak with Ronald Reagan, the government aggressively pursued the so-called War on Drugs and decided that arrest and incarceration would be the best method to keep people from using drugs. It is safe to say that that did not work very well at all, except to massively inflate the number of people in prison for nonviolent drug charges.

The second answer is harsh sentencing. The USA has more severe laws than many other developed countries. For instance, many states have three strikes laws, which make it difficult if not impossible to avoid a life sentence if convicted of a third felony—even one as minor as marijuana possession—after one has already had two serious or violent felonies. Mandatory minimum sentences mean that offenders have to serve long sentences, regardless of extenuating circumstances. Nonviolent crimes that in other countries would get drug treatment, a fine, or community service are punished in America with prison time.

A third answer is that the prison-industrial complex is a self-perpetuating system. If one has to spend more money on prisons—

and they always have to spend more money on prisons—that's less money available for prevention or rehabilitation. Parole officers and social workers are overworked and underfunded; drug treatment programs are not available for those who need them; schools decay and graduate students that are barely literate, much less capable of working a non-criminal job. In addition, prisons create a perfect environment to turn nonviolent offenders into violent offenders: they traumatize inmates with violence and rape and teach them to be brutal and never show vulnerability, because only the strong survive. Contacts on the inside can make crime easier on the outside. Being a convicted felon can make it incredibly difficult to get a job, especially in poor communities where jobs are scarce to begin with. The only option left is crime.

Who Benefits from the Prison-Industrial Complex?

The most important question to ask about any injustice is *cui bono?*—that is, who benefits? The answer, for the prison-industrial complex, is depressingly many people.

Consider government officials. Prosecutors and DAs are reelected based on how many convictions they get and criminals are off the streets and are willing to use tactics like unethical plea deals to make it happen. Law enforcement and corrections officials both benefit from there being more people in prison. More prisoners means more prisons and more funding and more jobs for corrections officials; more criminals means more arrests and more funding and more jobs for police officers. Tough-on-crime politicians get reelected: after all, "I dislike crime" is almost as uncontroversial an opinion as "I like puppies." Any politician who objects to the human rights abuses or ineffective tactics is smeared as a wimp whose election will lead to your children being murdered in their beds.

Or consider corporations. Prisons are a big business. In 2010 the states spent $39 billion on prisons, nearly all of which is going directly into the pockets of corporations. Food service? Corporation. Barbed wire? Corporation. Security cameras?

Corporation. Padded cells? You guessed it, a corporation. Building new prisons? Corporation (and given that a new prison can cost up to a hundred million dollars, a fairly profitable one at that). Some states have decided to cut out the middleman and just give the money directly to corporations, via allowing private prisons, which are run by for-profit companies and are responsible for 6% of state prisoners, 16% of federal prisoners, and half of all immigration prisoners. The private prison companies talk about their ability to "cut prices," which is a euphemism for poor conditions and not offering even the slightest attempts at rehabilitation. Of course, the states somehow have to fund all this: fortunately, investment banks are happy to loan to the states with interest, a highly profitable deal.

The media benefits as well: "if it bleeds it leads," after all. Increasing media coverage of crimes has lead to the illusion that we're less safe than ever, despite historically low crime rates. TV shows like *Law and Order* and its innumerable spinoffs are essentially propaganda for the police, who are depicted as noble, always-right crusaders battling against a world full of evil.

But perhaps the saddest people who benefit are rural communities. Prisons are typically placed in small towns, where they provide a revitalizing boost of jobs and money into a town that, with the loss of its manufacturing, probably has neither. "Corrections official" is one of the few well-paying middle-class jobs available for blue-collar workers, and the money they spend can save an entire dying small town. This shows you how the kyriarchy pits marginalized people against each other. In order to hold on and make a decent life for themselves, poor people have to f*** over other poor people.

Ultimately, the motivation behind the prison-industrial complex is simple: money. Crime and prisons are big business. The media increases its market share; rural communities get all-too-scarce good jobs; government agencies get more funding; politicians are re-elected; corporations earn billions of dollars in profit. As long as the status quo enriches some people, they're going to perpetuate the f***ed-up system. Private prison companies spend plenty of money lobbying for harsher sentencing laws. The nature of the incentives in place means they'd be fools not to.

Why Is this a Social Justice Issue?

So all that's unfortunate, but there are lots of unfortunate things that aren't social justice issues. What makes this a social justice concern and not simply a civil liberties violation like Internet censorship or consumer privacy? Because the prison-industrial complex systematically fucks over marginalized groups.

People of color are far more likely to be imprisoned. Sixty percent of prisoners are people of color. One in three black men can expect to go to prison in their lifetime. Black offenders receive sentences ten percent longer than white offenders. Although all races use drugs at approximately the same rate, people of color are far more likely to be arrested; although African Americans represent 14% of regular drug users, they're 37% of those arrested for drug use.

Immigration is an issue of particular concern. Obviously, the deportation of undocumented immigrants shows the privilege that people with citizenship have over people without citizenship. The immigration process itself favors those with class, education, and straight privilege. In addition, "show us your papers" laws and deportation disproportionately affect Hispanics, far more so than Asian or European undocumented immigrants.

Mentally ill people are also more likely to be imprisoned. 56% of state prisoners and 45% of federal prisoners have symptoms or a recent history of mental health problems. Prisoners have a two to four times higher rate of mental illness. 8 to 19 percent of prisoners have a mental illness to the point that it's a disability, and 15 to 20 percent will require psychiatric intervention during incarceration.

Class also plays a huge role in the justice system. If you're rich, you can hire a great lawyer. If you're poor, you get an overworked public defender who is going to pressure you to plea-bargain, which means that you're going to spend time in prison. Not to mention that crimes committed by poor people, such as burglary, are punished much more harshly than crimes committed by rich people (how many prosecutions were there in the case of the Wall Street people who committed massive fraud and wrecked the economy again?).

And why is this a concern for the Good Men Project? Because those people of color, those immigrants, those mentally ill people, those poor people… they're *mostly men*. Although the incarceration rate for women has increased in recent years, only 113,462 of the people in prison are female, less than 7.5%. Overwhelmingly, the population of prisons is male, and the most vulnerable men at that.

The greatest ally the prison-industrial complex has is denial. It is, by design, very easy to simply not think about how many Americans are in prison or on parole, or what that might mean about the state of our society; it is very easy to think that when you vote for tough-on-crime policies you're voting for cops and safe streets, not broken-down inner city schools and overcrowded prisons. Not thinking about it is how most people approach the problem, and it works very well. Pretending the prison-industrial complex doesn't exist will not alter their profit margins or their business models one iota, and that's how it's supposed to work.

> *"So clearly, some people are making lots and lots of money off the booming business of keeping human beings in cages."*

Some People Are Getting Rich off the Prison Industrial Complex

Ray Downs

In the following viewpoint Ray Downs argues that some people are making a lot of money off the prison industrial complex since many prisons in the United States are run by for-profit corporations. The author researched, and in some cases interviewed, the specific individuals who are most invested financially in the US private prison system. Ray Downs is a staff writer at the Broward/Palm Beach New Times, *where he works on investigative pieces. His work has appeared online in* Vice, The Atlantic, *and other news publications.*

As you read, consider the following questions:

1. How does prison privatization lead to the entrenchment of the prison industrial complex in American society?
2. Who are the main individuals cited by the author who have made fortunes off of prisons?
3. Why does the author state that "probably you" are also invested in the prison industrial complex?

Y ou likely already know how overcrowded and abusive the US prison system is, and you probably are also aware that the US has more people in prison than even China or Russia. In this age of privatization, of course, it's also not surprising that many of the detention centers are not actually operated by the government, but by for-profit companies. So clearly, some people are making lots and lots of money off the booming business of keeping human beings in cages.

But who are these people?

Using NASDAQ data, I looked through the long list of investors in Corrections Corporation of America and GEO Group, the two biggest corporations that operate detention centers in the US, to find out who was cashing in the most on prisons. When we say "prison-industrial complex," this is who we're talking about.

Henri Wedell

The individual who's invested the most in private prisons is Henri Wedell, who started serving on CCA's board of directors in 2000, when the company was struggling with scandals related to prisoner abuse and mismanagement. He now owns more than 650,000 shares in the company, which is far more successful these days. Those shares are worth more than $25 million.

I called Wedell to ask him what it was like to make a fortune from the incarceration of others, and whether it bothered him to profit off a system that puts more people in prison than any other country in the world.

"America is the freest country in the world," he told me. "America allows more freedom than any other country in the world, much more than Russia and a whole lot more than Scandinavia, where they really aren't free. So offering all this freedom to society, there'll be a certain number of people, more in this country than elsewhere, who take advantage of that freedom, abuse it, and end up in prison. That happens because we are so free in this country."

Presumably, when he's referring to all the freedom Americans have, he's not including the 80,000 inmates in 60 prisons operated by CCA.

George Zoley

Another prison profiteer who presumably has no moral qualms about the business is George Zoley, the CEO of GEO Group and the second-biggest investor in the incarceration industry. In fact, he's so proud of his business, which has committed a laundry list of human rights abuses, he tried to get a college football stadium named after it.

Zoley made nearly $6 million last year through salary and bonuses alone, but the real money is in stocks—he owns more than 500,000 shares in GEO, and he has made $23 million in stock trades during one 18-month period. But you can't accuse him of not earning his pay, exactly. GEO saw a 56 percent spike in profits in the first quarter of 2013, and the company's executives reassured investors that the incarceration rate wouldn't be dropping any time soon when announcing its earnings. Zoley will be mega rich for years to come.

Jeremy Mindich and Matt Sirovich

Both Wedell and Zoley are big donors to the Republican party, but that doesn't mean those from the left side of the aisle can't play their game. Matt Sirovich and Jeremy Mindich both donate to Democratic politicians and are involved with progressive-leaning organizations like Root Capital, a nonprofit lending company that offers loans to farmers in developing countries to alleviate poverty.

Their day job, however, is running Scopia Capital, a hedge fund that is one of the largest shareholders of GEO Group. The fund owns about $300 million in shares in that company, which represents 12 percent of its entire portfolio. Like Zoley, they are good at what they do—their fund outperformed the market by 20 percentage points, and the State of New Jersey hired Scopia to manage $150 million worth of pensions.

CORPORATIONS THAT BENEFIT FROM THE PIC

Prison labor in the United States is referred to as insourcing. Under the Work Opportunity Tax Credit (WOTC), employers receive a tax credit of $2,400 for every work-release inmate they employ as a reward for hiring "risky target groups."

The workers are not only cheap labor, but they are considered easier to control. They also tend to be African-American males. Companies are free to avoid providing benefits like health insurance or sick days.

According to the *Left Business Observer*, "the federal prison industry produces 100 percent of all military helmets, war supplies and other equipment. The workers supply 98 percent of the entire market for equipment assembly services; 93 percent of paints and paintbrushes; 92 percent of stove assembly; 46 percent of body armor; 36 percent of home appliances; 30 percent of headphones/microphones/speakers; and 21 percent of office furniture."

With all of that productivity, the inmates make about 90 cents to $4 a day.

Here are some of the biggest corporations to use such practices, but there are hundreds more:

McDonald's

McDonald's uses inmates to produce frozen foods. Inmates process beef for patties.

Wendy's

Wendy's has also been identified as relying on prison labor to reduce its cost of operations. Inmates also process beef for patties.

Wal-Mart

The company uses inmates for manufacturing purposes. The company "hires" inmates to clean products of UPC bar codes so that products can be resold.

Starbucks

The company uses inmates to cut costs as well. Starbucks subcontractor Signature Packaging Solutions hired Washington state prisoners to package holiday coffees.

Sprint

Inmates provide telecommunication services. Inmates are used in call centers.

Verizon

Inmates provide telecommunication services.

Victoria's Secret

The company uses inmates to cut production costs. In South Carolina, female inmates were used to sew products. Also, inmates reportedly have been used to replace "made in" tags with "Made in USA" tags.

Fidelity Investments

401(K) or other investments are held by Fidelity, and, in some cases, some of your money invested by Fidelity is used for prison labor or in other operations related to the prison industrial complex. The investment firm funds the American Legislative Exchange Council (ALEC), which has created laws authorizing and increasing the use of inmates in manufacturing.

J.C Penney and Kmart

Kmart and J.C. Penney both sell jeans made by inmates in Tennessee prisons.

American Airlines and Avis

American Airlines and the car rental company Avis use inmates to take reservations.

"12 Corporations Benefit from Prison Industrial Complex," by Rick Riley, popularresistance.org, July 7, 2015.

I called them up to ask their thoughts about being politically liberal but heavily invested in private prisons, but Mindich refused to answer any questions and Sirovich was unavailable.

It should be pointed out that while being far to the left politically might seem incompatible with investing in prisons (or managing a hedge fund in the first place), the Democratic party is totally fine with the incarceration rate. Although Richard Nixon and Ronald Reagan are largely responsible for the drug-war policies that caused the prison population to skyrocket, Bill Clinton was a "tough on crime" president who continued their ideas. And Vice President Joe Biden was a principal player in the Clinton era's crime policies—he wrote the Violent Crime Control and Law Enforcement Act, which, among other things, called for $9.7 billion in increased funding for prisons and stiffer penalties for drug offenders.

Though the US prison population is shrinking slightly, the number of inmates in federal lockup is increasing, and while Obama keeps saying he's ending the war on drugs, he's also proposed budgets that call for increasing the amount of money spent on the Bureau of Prisons. So it's not such a stretch that a Democratic donor would also be in the men-in-cages industry.

Retired People and Probably You

The Vanguard Group and Fidelity Investments are America's top two 401(k) providers. They are also two of the private prison industry's biggest investors.

Together, they own about 20 percent of both CCA and GEO. That means if you have a 401(k) plan, there's a good chance you benefit financially from private prisons. And even if you don't, there are many more mutual funds, brokerage firms, and banks that invest in private prisons—it being a growth industry and all—so if you have money somewhere other than your wallet or your mattress, it's a good bet you're involved in some way with companies that are locking up and probably abusing inmates.

This is especially true for government employees like public school teachers because their retirement funds are some of the biggest investors in private prisons. According to NASDAQ data, the retirement funds for public employees and teachers in New York and California together have about $60 million ($30 million each) invested in CCA and GEO. Teacher retirement funds in Texas and Kentucky have $8.3 million and $4 million invested in prisons respectively, and public employees in Florida ($10.3 million), Ohio ($8.6 million), Texas ($5.6 million), Arizona ($5.3 million), and Colorado ($2.25 million) are also connected to the industry. Except for New York, which has only one privately run detention facility, each of these states has several prisons run by CCA and GEO Group facilities. And it's not just Americans who have ties to prisons. Foreign investors have money in them as well, including the pension fund for the Royal Canadian Mounted Police, which recently sold off its $5.1 million worth of GEO Group stock.

Most of these employees are probably unaware that their pensions are tied to prisons—and it's hard to say that these are "bad" investments from a purely capitalistic perspective, since these prisons are making money hand over fist. The private prison industry is entrenched in our society. And the only way to make sure that we're not individually and collectively profiting off of it is to close these things.

> *"The prison industrial complex is fed by a surveillance culture that targets people of color, and in particular men. Some examples are the racist stop-and-frisk policy in New York, the phenomenon of driving while black or brown, and the three-strikes policies that funnel non-violent offenders into maximum security prison systems."*

America's Prison Industrial Complex Is Modern-Day Slavery

Sezin Koehler

In the following viewpoint, Sezin Koehler examines how people of color are disproportionately targeted and affected by the prison industrial complex, resulting in what is essentially a form of modern-day slavery. The author compares the prison industrial complex with slavery in terms of the economic profits it generates, high recidivism rates, violence, inhumane conditions, and systematic demoralization. Sezin Koehler is a writer whose work has been featured in Al Jazeera, Huffington Post, Jezebel, Think Progress, and Buzzfeed, among others.

"A Primer on the Prison Industrial Complex in America," by Sezin Koehler, Wear Your Voice, September 3, 2017. Reprinted by permission.

As you read, consider the following questions:

1. What are some of the ways people of color are disproportionally targeted by the prison industrial complex?
2. What are some ways that an individual may find himself or herself subjected to incarceration besides committing a capital crime?
3. Why does the author compare the prison industrial complex to modern-day slavery?

A t the confluence of capitalism, racism, and mass-scale sadism we find what is known as the prison industrial complex, a complicated socio-cultural system that keeps America's prisons full and predominantly with inmates of color. The term prison industrial complex was coined by activist scholar Angela Davis in a speech-turned-essay for ColorLines in 1997 to describe the veritable pipeline of young men of color subsumed into an archaic and unyielding prison system, often for the entirety of their lives.

In *Masked Racism: Reflections on the Prison Industrial Complex* Angela Davis writes:

"[P]risons do not disappear problems, they disappear human beings. And the practice of disappearing vast numbers of people from poor, immigrant, and racially marginalized communities has literally become big business."

And:

"To deliver up bodies destined for profitable punishment, the political economy of prisons relies on racialized assumptions of criminality—such as images of black welfare mothers reproducing criminal children—and on racist practices in arrest, conviction, and sentencing patterns. Colored bodies constitute the main human raw material in this vast experiment to disappear the major social problems of our time. Once the aura of magic is stripped away from the imprisonment solution, what is revealed is racism, class bias, and the parasitic seduction

PRISON FOOD

In the popular imagination, prison food is disgusting. The images crop up in films and TV shows as unidentifiable cafeteria slop or a sweaty slab of bologna on two pieces of white bread shoved through a cell door.

But the reality is sometimes even worse.

Incarcerated people are six times more likely to contract foodborne illnesses than people on the outside. Across the country, prisoners complain of hunger, sometimes intense enough that it drives them to eat toothpaste and toilet paper. They have been served rancid chicken, food infested with maggots, cake that was nibbled on by rats. Problems with food—both in terms of quantity and quality—have been the basis of prison riots throughout history.

To be fair, running a prison kitchen is no simple task. Staff oversee dozens of inmate kitchen workers and feed hundreds or thousands of prisoners at every meal.

But according to some prisoner advocates and prison workers, one of the biggest reasons for the problems is privatization.

Many state prison systems, in an effort to cut costs, have stopped providing their own food services and instead contract out to private companies. This is part of a growing trend toward prison privatization in general.

of capitalist profit. The prison industrial system materially and morally impoverishes its inhabitants and devours the social wealth needed to address the very problems that have led to spiraling numbers of prisoners."

What are some of the things that constitute our social construction of crime and criminal behavior? We have extreme cases of violence, murder, theft, rape and sexual assault. But homelessness is also coded as criminal. Being undocumented in America is also a crime. Addiction often leads to incarceration, as do untreated mental health problems due to a lack of state psychiatric facilities and hospitals. The intersection of poverty,

Private providers have a business incentive to keep costs as low as possible. That results in lower-quality food, says Tim Thielman, food service administrator at the Ramsey County Correctional Facility in St. Paul, Minn., and the immediate past president of the Association of Correctional Food Service Affiliates.

"What it comes down to is whether it's a self-operated facility or one that's run by a contracted feeder," he says. "You look at those companies, and they're in it to make a profit. I don't want to talk bad about the companies, but it's about money to them, and if there are ways that they can feed [prisoners] products that are lesser quality, [they will]."

Prison reform advocates agree, expressing general reservations about privatization as a cost-saving measure.

"The problem with the privatization of anything in the prison context is that the market forces that we rely on in the rest of society don't operate in prisons. There's no consumer choice" says David Fathi, the national prison project director for the American Civil Liberties Union. "If a prisoner doesn't like the food, he can't just go somewhere else and put the company out of business."

"Maggots with a Side of Dirt? What Privatization Does to Prison Food," by Natalie Delgadillo, Governing, February 1, 2018.

race, and lack of access to education and social resources are also direct lines into the vortex that is the prison industrial complex.

The prison industrial complex is fed by a surveillance culture that targets people of color, and in particular men. Some examples are the racist stop-and-frisk policy in New York, the phenomenon of driving while black or brown, and the three-strikes policies that funnel non-violent offenders into maximum security prison systems. Once you have been incarcerated and released, your disenfranchisement begins: Ex-cons are not permitted to vote, which is reminiscent of slavery eras when people of color had no voice in the American political system. There are currently

6 million black Americans in this country who are not permitted to vote because of felony disenfranchisement.

In fact, the Prison Industrial Complex has quite a great deal in common with slavery, especially since the privatization of prisons as a capitalist industry is now more the norm than the exception. Prison labor is a cheap source for big business, and these multi-million dollar companies profit off the backs of mostly men of color. That these companies are predominantly run by white men only adds to the disgusting parallels of the American prison system and slavery of old. Not to mention all the other people and organizations who profit off the metaphorical highways into the Prison Industrial Complex, such as the bail bond industry and monopolies on inmate access to communication services such as telephones and the internet.

While in theory prisons were created in order to rehabilitate criminals, in practice it is quite exactly the opposite. Extremely high recidivism rates—the rates at which former inmates are re-incarcerated—indicate that time on the inside only further hardens criminal behavior when back on the outside. Violence in prison, and in particular sexual violence, further strips prisoners of their dignity and the lack of treatment for mental health issues after surviving rape(s) only contributes to breaking inmates in fundamental ways that keep them entrenched in the prison industrial complex. Prison wardens and guards often use draconian corporal punishment methods and extended solitary confinement bouts to make their prisoners more malleable while incarcerated, but these brutal techniques create chain reactions of psychological trauma that prevent a person often from even conceiving of a life outside of crime.

Many non-violent offenders are placed in maximum security prisons in order to bolster the profits of businesses that capitalize off prison labor, and these inmates are particularly vulnerable to the horrific social conditions in prison that manufacture criminals instead of rehabilitating them. HBO's miniseries *The Night Of* demonstrates perfectly how entrance into the prison industrial complex even as an innocent defendant will shift a life trajectory into one of crime from the inside to the outside.

The prison industrial complex is an intricate and pervasive system with a sole function of generating profits off the backs of people of color while simultaneously dismantling the very humanity of people who are caught in its monstrous rabbit hole to ensure their longevity in that structure. And so long as there is money to be made—and especially in private prisons that do not operate under standard state prison procedures—various state and governmental arms will continue to replenish prison coffers with people to work. After all, owners of private prisons are huge political donors and the prison industrial complex is a comprehensive top-to-bottom socio-political system that ensures profitability while trampling on human rights.

Because ultimately, the end goal of the prison industrial complex is for a small group of (mostly white) men to make money off of the targeting, oppression, and incarceration of large communities of (mostly brown and black) men. Currently, the prison industrial complex is responsible for not only the inhumane treatment of humans who are supposedly endowed with a set of inalienable rights per the USA's constitution, but also to their socio-cultural and even psychological positioning as pathological dangers to American society.

In a nutshell, the prison industrial complex is indeed modern-day American slavery. And under Trump, it is only getting worse.

"*The Prison Industry Enhancement Certification Program (PIECP)—allows inmates to work for a private employer in a 'free world' occupation and earn the prevailing wage.*"

Prison Work Programs Are Beneficial

Marilyn C. Moses and Cindy J. Smith, PhD

In the following viewpoint, authors Marilyn C. Moses and Cindy J. Smith argue that the historic mainstay of prison life, where inmates engage in labor of some sort while incarcerated, has broad benefits for both society and those incarcerated indivduals who participate in prison work programs. One such benefit is that former inmates can more easily find employment when discharged because they have been trained to perform specific tasks. Marilyn C. Moses has been a social science analyst at the National Institute of Justice for over 28 years and holds an M.S. degree in criminal justice. Cindy J. Smith is former director of the United Nations Interregional Crime and Justice Research Institute (UNICRI).

"Factories Behind Fences: Do Prison Real Work Programs Work?" by Marilyn C. Moses and Cindy J. Smith, PhD, US Department of Justice, June 1, 2007.

As you read, consider the following questions:

1. Does the fact that the authors are writing for the US Department of Justice make a difference in your interpretation of the viewpoint?
2. What is the PIECP program?
3. According to the viewpoint, are prison work programs successful in preventing inmate recidivism?

When someone is in prison, does having a real job with real pay yield benefits when he or she is released? Findings from an evaluation funded by the National Institute of Justice (NIJ) suggest that this might be the case.

Offenders who worked for private companies while imprisoned obtained employment more quickly, maintained employment longer, and had lower recidivism rates than those who worked in traditional correctional industries or were involved in "other-than-work" (OTW) activities.

"Factories behind fences" is not a new idea. Traditional industries (TI)—in which offenders are supervised by corrections staff and work for a modest sum—have been a mainstay of corrections for more than 150 years. Examples of traditional industries include the manufacture of signs, furniture, and garments, as well as the stereotypical license plates. By obtaining work experience in these industries, inmates acquire the skills they need to secure gainful employment upon release and avoid recidivism.

Another program—the Prison Industry Enhancement Certification Program (PIECP)—allows inmates to work for a private employer in a "free world" occupation and earn the prevailing wage. Created by Congress in 1979, PIECP encourages State and local correctional agencies to form partnerships with private companies to give inmates real work opportunities.[1] Over the years, PIECP operations have included the manufacture of aluminum screens and windows for Solar Industries, Inc.; circuit boards for Joint Venture Electronics; street sweeper brushes for

United Rotary Brush Corporation; corrugated boxes for PRIDE Box; gloves for Hawkeye Glove Manufacturing, Inc.; and the manufacture and refurbishment of Shelby Cobra automobiles for Shelby American Management Co. Other PIECP operations include alfalfa production for Five Dot Land and Cattle Company; papaya packing for Tropical Hawaiian Products; potato processing for Floyd Wilcox & Sons; and boat-building for Misty Harbor.

PIECP seeks to:

- Generate products and services that enable prisoners to make a contribution to society, offset the cost of incarceration, support family members, and compensate crime victims.
- Reduce prison idleness, increase inmate job skills, and improve the prospects for prisoners' successful transition to the community upon release.

More than 70,000 inmates—an average of 2,500 per year—have participated in PIECP since the program's inception. By the end of 2005, 6,555 offenders were employed in the program. Although this number reflects a 285 percent increase in PIECP positions in the past decade, it represents only a small fraction of the total number of inmates in our Nation's State prisons and local jails.

Does the Program Work?

In a sense, PIECP can be thought of as a grand experiment. After 28 years, the obvious question is: Does it work?

To find out, NIJ teamed with the US Department of Justice's Bureau of Justice Assistance to fund the first national evaluation of PIECP. Researchers at the University of Baltimore compared a group of postrelease inmates who worked in PIECP with inmates from two other groups—those who worked in TI and those involved in OTW activities, including idleness.[2] Cindy J. Smith, Ph.D., one of the authors of this article, was part of that research team. Then at the University of Baltimore, Smith and her colleagues considered two questions:

- Does PIECP participation increase postrelease employment more than work in TI and OTW programs?
- Does PIECP participation reduce recidivism more than work in TI or OTW programs?

Although the findings are not conclusive, they are positive. (See end section, "A Word of Caution: Selection Bias.") Researchers found that, after they were released, PIECP participants found jobs more quickly and held them longer than did their counterparts in the TI and OTW groups. Approximately 55 percent of PIECP workers obtained employment within the first quarter after release. Only 40 percent of their counterparts found employment within that time.

Nearly 49 percent of PIECP participants were employed continuously for more than 1 year, whereas 40.4 percent of the offenders in TI and 38.5 percent of the offenders in OTW programs were continuously employed for that length of time.

Three years out, PIECP participants performed better than releasees from the TI or OTW groups. Almost 14 percent of PIECP releasees were employed for 3 continuous years, but only 10.3 percent of the other offenders maintained constant employment for that same period of time.

Examining wages earned by the participants after they were released, the researchers found that the PIECP group earned more than the TI and OTW groups. Of all the releasees, however, 55 percent did not earn wages equal to a full-time job at the Federal minimum wage. Because the data available to the researchers reported total earnings only and not the number of hours worked, it was impossible to determine whether this was because the releasees were: (1) working part-time, (2) working intermittently, or (3) earning less than the Federal minimum wage.

Recidivism

The researchers measured recidivism rates for all three groups using the traditional yardsticks: new arrest, conviction, and incarceration.[3] The results showed that PIECP releasees had lower rates of rearrest, conviction, and incarceration than offenders who were in the TI or the OTW groups.

At the end of the first year postrelease, 82 percent of PIECP participants were arrest free. The average amount of time from release to first arrest for PIECP participants was approximately 993 days (slightly less than 3 years). At 1 year postrelease, offenders in the TI and OTW groups remained arrest free at approximately the same rate (77 percent and 76 percent, respectively) as PIECP participants. By 3 years out, however, the arrest-free rates for all three groups declined to 60 percent for the PIECP participants and 52 percent for offenders in the TI and OTW programs.

Looking at conviction and reincarceration rates, the researchers found that 77 percent of PIECP participants were conviction free during the followup periods, compared to 73 percent of the OTW group. Ninety-three percent of PIECP participants remained incarceration free during the followup periods, compared to 89 percent of the OTW participants.

Inmate PIECP Wages

Wages earned by PIECP participants in prison benefit taxpayers in addition to helping the inmates themselves. Although the program requires a percentage of PIECP wages to be saved to assist the inmate when he is released, the remaining wages make their way back into the national economy, either directly or indirectly. A significant portion of the wages earned by prisoners in the program, for example, goes directly to the State to cover the cost of prisoner room and board. PIECP wages also provide child support and alimony to family members, as well as restitution to crime victims.

An Underutilized Rehabilitation Option?

The research suggests that PIECP has been successful. Inmate PIECP wages benefit inmates, taxpayers, victims, families, and States. PIECP participants also acquire postrelease jobs more quickly, retain these jobs longer, and return to the criminal justice system less frequently and at a lower rate than inmates who worked in traditional industries or engaged in other-than-work activities. These findings suggest that PIECP is an underutilized rehabilitation option and that additional efforts to increase the number of PIECP jobs could have an important impact on the Nation's prison and jail populations.

A Word of Caution: Selection Bias

Although the results of the Prison Industry Enhancement Certification Program (PIECP) study are positive—showing better outcomes for participants in the PIECP group compared to the traditional industries (TI) and the other-than-work (OTW) groups—they do not definitively show that the better outcomes were due to PIECP itself. This is because the participants in the three groups were not randomly assigned to the groups, a process that ensures that the differences in results are due to the program, rather than to preexisting differences among the participants.

How then were participants in this study assigned to the different groups? First, prisoners volunteered to participate in a work program. They were then interviewed by prospective employers in both the TI program and PIECP. Therefore, inmates who worked in either the TI program or PIECP were "self-selected" and may have had different motivations and backgrounds than the OTW inmates, the third group studied, which may have led to better outcomes. This concern, known as selection bias, can be definitively ruled out only by random assignment to groups that are going to be compared. In this study, selection bias seems a larger concern when comparing the volunteers (that is, PIECP and TI participants) to the non-volunteers (the OTW group) than in comparing the results of the two employment (PIECP and TI) groups.

The researchers in this study attempted to ensure that the groups were comparable by matching inmates in the three groups using a number of factors, including demographics and time served. Nevertheless, this matching may not have completely eliminated the selection bias. Therefore, the results should be interpreted with caution.

Endnotes

1. With the exception of PIECP, US jail and prison inmates are prohibited, under the Amhurst-Sumners Act of 1935, from producing goods for sale in open interstate commercial markets; PIECP-certified programs are exempt from the $10,000 limit on the sale of prisoner-made goods to the Federal Government.
2. The sample size included 6,464 inmates, with subjects nearly equally divided among groups. The sample included offenders released from 46 prisons in 5 States that implemented PIECP from January 1, 1996, to June 30, 2001. The followup period began on the day the inmate was released and ranged from slightly under 2 years to 7.5 years.
3. Technical violations were not considered new arrests.

| "The criminal justice system is not broken because there are too many people in private prisons. It is broken because there are too many people in prison, period."

Privatization Isn't the Problem. Too Many Are Being Incarcerated.

Robby Soave

In the following viewpoint, Robby Soave argues that left-leaning prison reformers are making a mistake by simply focusing on canceling private prison contracts. This is because most inmates are serving time in government prisons, the author writes, and the problem of over-incarceration has deeper roots. Robby Soave is a senior editor at Reason.com. His work has appeared in The New York Times, The Daily Beast, *and* US News and World Report.

As you read, consider the following questions:

1. What is the main problem regarding anti-privatization politics and the prison industrial complex?
2. Who is the author primarily criticizing?
3. How does the author see reformers as missing the point? What is he proposing instead?

"The Justice Department Is Wrong. Private Prisons Aren't the Problem," by Robby Soave, Reason Foundation, August 18, 2016 Reason.com and Reason magazine. Reprinted by permission.

Liberal critics of the US criminal justice system overwhelming cheered the Justice Department's recent decision to cancel federal contracts with private prisons. Their enthusiasm for this misguided half-measure is disappointing and betrays a fundamental misunderstanding of the real problem.

The criminal justice system is not broken because there are too many people in private prisons. It is broken because there are too many people in prison, period. Merely shuffling prisoners from one form of captivity to another might be an exciting development for lefties whose driving force is hatred of corporations and profits, but the move won't accomplish much else. It may even make life even more uncomfortable for the actual prisoners.

If left-leaning reformers understand this, many of them aren't letting on. Black Lives Matter activist Shaun King hailed the Justice Department's decision as a "huge deal." Ilyse Hogue, the president of NARAL, called it "one of the most significant victories of the decade." California's Democratic Attorney General Kamala Harris said that she applauds the decision. "Mass incarceration should not be incentivized by private gain."

This analysis is ahistorical. Private prisons did not create the conditions that encouraged mass incarceration—private prisons came into being as a response to mass incarceration.

As Reason's C.J. Ciaramella points out, the federal Bureau of Prisons started contracting with private corporations in 1997. The government took this step to help alleviate overcrowding, having arrested and imprisoned huge swaths of the population as a response to public panic stemming from the crime wave of the 1980s and early '90s. Incarcerating so many people was an overreaction to the problem—it was bad public policy, and terribly costly. The rise of private prisons is a symptom of this mistake and getting rid of them without addressing the underlying condition that made them necessary in the first place is counter-productive to the cause of criminal justice reform.

Where are these federal prisoners going to go? Back to publicly-run prisons? It might very well be the case that further overcrowding of public prisons is the consequence of closing private prisons. While it may delight liberals to know that private companies aren't making money off of prisoners' misery anymore, the prisoners will still be, well, prisoners. They might even be more miserable, living in more closely confined quarters and competing with even more inmates for prison resources.

The Justice Department claims that it reviewed its private prisons and found them lacking. "They simply do not provide the same level of correctional services, programs, and resources; they do not save substantially on costs; and as noted in a recent report by the Department's Office of Inspector General, they do not maintain the same level of safety and security," wrote Deputy Attorney General Sally Yates, according to *The Washington Post*. This matches the public perception of private prisons. The media routinely portrays them as less safe: the most recent season of *Orange Is the New Black* insists that privatization is nothing short of a humanitarian crisis for inmates, and *Mother Jones* garnered universal acclaim for an investigative report on the inadequacies of a private prison in Louisiana.

No one disagrees that private prisons have huge problems, are often mismanaged, and frequently neglect inmates' safety. But public prisons are plagued by the exact same problems. It's not clear that one kind is clearly better run than the other. And private prisons have at least one important advantage over public prisons: it's easier to hold management responsible when management is someone other than the government. As Reason's Leonard Gilroy and Adrian Moore observed, "If dissatisfied with performance, a government can cancel a prison contract with a private company. By contrast, the government tends not to fire itself, and the watchmen ultimately watch themselves."

Concerns that private corporations will pack their prisons as tightly as possible in order to take in more inmates—and thus, more funds—are legitimate. But public prisons have worrisome incentives, too. Unions representing prison guards, for instance, want their prisons overflowing: they want to protect their members' jobs.

Keep in mind that the overwhelming majority of prisoners—state *and* federal prisoners—are locked up in a public prison. Private prisons hold just about 10 percent of all inmates. The Justice Department's order only applies to federal prisoners, but even if it were expanded to cover all prisoners—a legally dubious move, to be sure—this just wouldn't be a very big slice of the pie.

But more importantly, what good would it do these prisoners, anyway? They will still be locked up, and that's the real public problem, not the manager overseeing their confinement.

Most federal prisoners in privately-run prisons, in fact, have violated immigration laws. If the federal government really wanted to do something for these people, it could enforce immigration laws differently and re-sentence prisoners. The US government should imprison fewer people whose only crime was trying to live in this country, and it should find ways to manage other criminals that do not require locking them up for decades. The government could, for instance, focus on rehabilitation and reducing recidivism. It could require prisons to develop programs to accomplish these priorities, with the ultimate goal of reducing the prison population (and potential prison population), saving money in the long run.

In reality, some state and local governments are already doing this—with private prisons. Pennsylvania, for instance, made reducing recidivism rates among prisoners a factor in determining compensation for private prisons. And governmental authorities in New York and Massachusetts are making creative use of private investment to achieve desirable prison goals.

Bernie Sanders wants to ban private prisons entirely, and many liberals apparently agree with him. (Democratic presidential candidate Hillary Clinton has merely stopped accepting campaign donations from corporations that run them.) It would take a lot of political effort to accomplish this, and it would be a huge waste. Private prisons aren't a problem—they are, like all prisons, the *symptom* of a problem (over-criminalization, over-enforcement, and over-incarceration) that all proponents of criminal justice reform should be working together to fix.

Periodical and Internet Sources Bibliography

The following articles have been selected to supplement the diverse views presented in this chapter.

Critical Resistance, "What Is the PIC? What Is Abolition?" http://criticalresistance.org/about/not-so-common-language/.

Angela Davis, "Masked Racism: Reflections on the Prison Industrial Complex," History Is a Weapon, https://www.historyisaweapon.com/defcon1/davisprison.html.

Diversity Inc, "The Prison Industrial Complex: Biased, Predatory and Growing," October 8, 2010, https://www.diversityinc.com/the-prison-industrial-complex-biased-predatory-and-growing/.

Empty Cages Collective, "What Is the Prison Industrial Complex?" http://www.prisonabolition.org/what-is-the-prison-industrial-complex/.

Eoin Higgins, "New Report Names Nearly 4,000 Companies Profiting Off of Private Prison Industry," Common Dreams, April 30, 2019, https://www.commondreams.org/news/2019/04/30/new-report-names-nearly-4000-companies-profiting-private-prison-industry.

Robert Longley, "What You Should Know About the Prison-Industrial Complex," Thoughtco.com, July 28, 2019, https://www.thoughtco.com/what-you-should-know-about-the-prison-industrial-complex-4155637.

Vicky Pelaez, "The Prison Industry in the United States: Big Business or a New Form of Slavery?" Global Research, December 15, 2019, https://www.globalresearch.ca/the-prison-industry-in-the-united-states-big-business-or-a-new-form-of-slavery/8289.

Romarilyn Ralston, "Revisiting the Prison Industrial Complex," Open Democracy, April 15, 2018, https://www.opendemocracy.net/en/revisiting-prison-industrial-complex/.

Worth Rises, "The Prison Industrial Complex: Mapping Private Sector Players," April, 2019, https://worthrises.org/picreport2019.

How Did We Get Here?

Chapter Preface

The private prison industry started to gain traction in the United States following President Richard Nixon's so-called War on Drugs. The legislation, passed in 1971, called for harsher sentencing for drug offenders, even low-level offenders.

Nixon's initiative was intended as a public health crusade. But through the years it became a punitive war that disproportionately hurt black communities. Private prisons flourished in part to keep up with rapid expansion and the need to contain and service incarcerated individuals.

The following chapter offers perspectives concentrating on the history and background of what we now call the prison industrial complex.

One viewpoint takes a statistical approach to present the War on Drugs as a failing campaign, displaying tangible data regarding the large numbers of people these laws and policies have affected.

Another argues that the War on Drugs is too often used as a scapegoat for mass incarceration and the prison population explosion of recent decades.

One viewpoint focuses on a particular individual who was incarcerated in a privately operated prison and the negative outcomes surrounding the man's situation.

Another shows how former president Bill Clinton's 1994 crime bill added to the institutionalization of racism and the further buildup of the prison industrial complex.

How did we get here? The answers are messy and complex, and not everyone agrees on them.

> "One-fifth of the incarcerated
> population—or
> 456,000 individuals—is serving
> time for a drug charge. Another
> 1.15 million people are on probation
> and parole for drug-related offenses."

The War on Drugs Was a Disastrous Policy

Betsy Pearl

In the following viewpoint Betsy Pearl presents a statistical analysis of the human consequences of the War on Drugs, a policy which can best be understood as leading up to—and in part causing—what we now call the prison industrial complex and the problems associated with it. The author notes that today, most experts agree that this policy was a failure and should be replaced with a more effective model. Betsy Pearl is senior policy analyst for Criminal Justice Reform at the Center for American Progress. She was formerly a policy adviser at the US Department of Justice.

As you read, consider the following questions:

1. What effect does incarceration have on public safety?
2. Why should drug abuse be treated as a public health issue, according to the author?
3. What are Law Enforcement Assisted Diversion (LEAD) programs?

"Ending the War on Drugs: By the Numbers," by Betsy Pearl, Center for American Progress, June 27, 2018. Reprinted by permission.

P resident Richard Nixon called for a war on drugs in 1971, setting in motion a tough-on-crime policy agenda that continues to produce disastrous results today. Policymakers at all levels of government passed harsher sentencing laws and increased enforcement actions, especially for low-level drug offenses. The consequences of these actions are magnified for communities of color, which are disproportionately targeted for enforcement and face discriminatory practices across the justice system. Today, researchers and policymakers alike agree that the war on drugs is a failure. This fact sheet summarizes research findings that capture the need to replace the war on drugs with a fairer, more effective model that treats substance misuse as a public health issue—not a criminal justice issue.

The War on Drugs

- Every 25 seconds, someone in America is arrested for drug possession. The number of Americans arrested for possession has tripled since 1980, reaching 1.3 million arrests per year in 2015—six times the number of arrests for drug sales.
- One-fifth of the incarcerated population—or 456,000 individuals—is serving time for a drug charge. Another 1.15 million people are on probation and parole for drug-related offenses.
- Incarcerating people for drug-related offenses has been shown to have little impact on substance misuse rates. Instead, incarceration is linked with increased mortality from overdose. In the first two weeks after their release from prison, individuals are almost 13 times more likely to die than the general population. The leading cause of death among recently released individuals is overdose. During that period, individuals are at a 129 percent greater risk of dying from an overdose than the general public.
- Incarceration has a negligible effect on public safety. Crime rates have trended downward since 1990, and researchers

attribute 75 to 100 percent of these reductions to factors other than incarceration.

Racial Disparities

- Black Americans are four times more likely to be arrested for marijuana charges than their white peers. In fact, black Americans make up nearly 30 percent of all drug-related arrests, despite accounting for only 12.5 percent of all substance users.
- Black Americans are nearly six times more likely to be incarcerated for drug-related offenses than their white counterparts, despite equal substance usage rates. Almost 80 percent of people serving time for a federal drug offense are black or Latino. In state prisons, people of color make up 60 percent of those serving time for drug charges.
- In the federal system, the average black defendant convicted of a drug offense will serve nearly the same amount of time (58.7 months) as a white defendant would for a violent crime (61.7 months).
- People of color account for 70 percent of all defendants convicted of charges with a mandatory minimum sentence. Prosecutors are twice as likely to pursue a mandatory minimum sentence for a black defendant than a white defendant charged with the same offense, and black defendants are less likely to receive relief from mandatory minimums. On average, defendants subject to mandatory minimums spend five times longer in prison than those convicted of other offenses.

Economic Impact

- Since 1971, the war on drugs has cost the United States an estimated $1 trillion. In 2015, the federal government spent an estimated $9.2 million every day to incarcerate people charged with drug-related offenses—that's more than $3.3 billion annually.

- State governments spent another $7 billion in 2015 to incarcerate individuals for drug-related charges. North Carolina, for example, spent more than $70 million incarcerating people for drug possession. And Georgia spent $78.6 million just to lock up people of color for drug offenses—1.6 times more than the state's budget current for substance use treatment services.
- In contrast, marijuana legalization would save roughly $7.7 billion per year in averted enforcement costs and would yield an additional $6 billion in tax revenue. The net total—$13.7 billion—could send more than 650,000 students to public universities every year.

The Opioid Epidemic

- In 2016, 11.8 million Americans misused prescription opioids or heroin. Around 3.6 percent of adolescents (ages 12 to 17) and 7.3 percent of young adults (ages 18 to 25) reported opioid misuse in the last year.
- Every 16 minutes, a person in America dies from an opioid overdose. In 2016, 42,249 Americans died from opioid overdoses—more than the number of people killed in motor vehicle accidents.
- Between 2014 and 2016, opioid overdose deaths increased by approximately 48 percent nationwide. Though whites have the highest rates of fatal opioid overdoses, fatalities are on the rise among communities of color. During the same period, opioid deaths rose by nearly 53 percent among Latinos and 84 percent among blacks.
- Americans account for less than 5 percent of the world's population but consume 80 percent of all opioids produced globally. Roughly 1 out of every 100 American adults—or 2.4 million people—have an opioid-use disorder.

PRISON IS NOT FOR PUNISHMENT IN SWEDEN

"Our role is not to punish. The punishment is the prison sentence: they have been deprived of their freedom. The punishment is that they are with us," says Nils Öberg, director-general of Sweden's prison and probation service.

Since 2004, Swedish prisoner numbers have fallen from 5,722 to 4,500 out of a population of 9.5 million, and last year four of the country's 56 prisons were closed and parts of other jails mothballed. In contrast, the prison population in England and Wales is 85,000 out of a population of 57 million.

With reoffending rates at about 40%—less than half of those in the UK and most other European countries—does he attribute this success to the country's effective policies on prisoner rehabilitation? "We obviously believe that it is part of the explanation; we hope we are doing something right. But it's going to be very difficult to prove that scientifically. We are increasing our efforts all the time," he says.

Last year a "national client survey" of several thousand Swedish prisoners was undertaken in order to identify the issues that have affected their criminal behaviour. "The survey did not bring up any surprises, but it gave us confirmation of what we have learned from experience—that it is not one problem that our clients face, but two or more, sometimes as many as seven or eight different ones, including perhaps drugs, alcohol and psychiatric problems. And these problems did not just appear overnight. These are things that have developed over years. Most of the sentences in this country are relatively short. The window of opportunity that we have to make a change is very small, so we need to start from day one. Our strategy is to cover the whole range of problems, not just the one problem."

[T]he implication in the Swedish model is that sentenced individuals are still primarily regarded as people with needs, to be assisted and helped.

"'Prison Is Not for Punishment in Sweden. We Get People into Better Shape,'" by Erwin James, Guardian News and Media Limited, November 26, 2014.

- The opioid epidemic costs the United States an estimated $504 billion per year, including the costs to the health care and justice systems as well as the economic impact of premature fatalities.
- Doctors wrote 259 million opiate prescriptions in 2012— enough for every American adult to have their own prescription, with 19 million to spare. Among women, prescription painkiller overdose deaths jumped 400 percent from 1999 to 2010.
- Opioid fatality rates jumped by 28 percent from 2015 to 2016, in large part due to a surge in overdoses on fentanyl—a synthetic opioid that is up to 50 times stronger than heroin. For the first time, synthetic opioids were the leading cause of all drug-related deaths, claiming some 20,000 lives in 2016 alone.

Impact of Interventions
Harm Reduction

- Many jurisdictions are reducing fatalities by expanding the availability of naloxone, an opioid overdose reversal drug. Every month, first responders in New York City save 180 lives by administering naloxone. A Massachusetts program reduced opioid-related deaths by 11 percent by distributing naloxone to individuals at risk of overdose, as well as to their family, friends, and service providers.
- Syringe access programs provide people with clean injection equipment to prevent syringe sharing, resulting in significant reductions in the incidence of blood-borne diseases. After implementing syringe access services, Washington state documented an 80 percent drop in new diagnoses of hepatitis B and hepatitis C. And in the District of Columbia, syringe access programs were credited with a 70 percent decrease in new HIV infections over two years, saving $44.3 million in lifetime health care costs. Nationally, researchers estimate

that syringe access programs yield a return on investment of $7.58 for every dollar spent.

- More than 60 international cities now operate supervised injection facilities (SIFs). SIFs are safe, hygienic places where individuals can inject preobtained drugs under medical supervision. These facilities have proven successful in connecting individuals with treatment and social services, as well as reducing overdose fatalities and blood-borne illnesses. Over the course of two years, a safe injection site in Vancouver, British Columbia, for example, was associated with a 35 percent reduction in overdose fatalities in its immediate vicinity. Safe injection sites also increased connections to substance use services. In the year after establishing the facility, Vancouver saw a 30 percent increase in entry into treatment among safe injection users, compared to the year before the site opened.
- A number of American cities—including Philadelphia, Seattle, and New York—are working to implement SIFs. Philadelphia estimated that SIFs would save up to 76 lives every year and avert up to 18 cases of HIV and 213 cases of hepatitis C. In New York, research found that SIFs would prevent an estimated 130 overdoses and save up to $7 million in health care costs annually.

Drug Courts

- Nationwide, there are more than 3,100 drug courts. These are specialized court programs that can reduce recidivism by sentencing defendants to substance use treatment, supportive services, and supervision and monitoring instead of incarceration. Interviews with drug court participants show significantly lower rates of reoffending (40 percent), as compared to comparison groups (53 percent). Specifically, drug court participation reduced future incidences of drug-related offenses, as well as property crimes.

- A longitudinal study of drug courts in Multnomah County, Oregon found that the program had long-lasting benefits. Fourteen years after enrolling in the program, drug court participants were 24 percent less likely to be rearrested for a drug-related offense and nearly 30 percent less likely to recidivate overall.
- A national evaluation of drug courts found that participants were 26 percent less likely to report substance use after completing the program than individuals processed through traditional judicial systems. Drug court participants were also less likely than nonparticipants to report unmet educational, employment, and financial service needs.
- Drug court completion rates vary significantly by program, ranging from 30 percent to 70 percent. The low completion rates among participants suggest that drug court programming may not provide the necessary support for some individuals. Successful graduation is also less common among communities of color. In some drug courts, failure rates for black participants exceed that of white participants by 30 percent or more. Notably, unsuccessful participants are often sentenced to long periods of incarceration, casting doubt on the model's capacity to reduce entanglement with the criminal justice system.

Law Enforcement Assisted Diversion

- Law Enforcement Assisted Diversion (LEAD) programs allow officers to divert individuals to treatment or social services, rather than making low-level drug arrests. The model was pioneered in Seattle, where it has yielded positive results. Individuals diverted through the LEAD program were 58 percent less likely to be rearrested, as compared to similar individuals processed through the criminal justice system.
- LEAD is associated with significant increases in housing and economic stability. After being referred to LEAD,

participants were 33 percent more likely to have an income or benefits, 46 percent more likely to be employed or in vocational training, and 89 percent more likely to obtain permanent housing, as compared to the month prior to referral. For every month individuals had stable housing, they were 17 percent less likely to be arrested. Every month of employment was associated with a 41 percent decrease in likelihood of arrest.

- On average, LEAD participants spent 39 fewer days in jail per year and were 87 percent less likely to be incarcerated in prison than comparison groups.
- For each participant, LEAD was associated with a $2,100 annual reduction in criminal and legal system costs. The average annual cost per nonparticipant increased by $5,961 in the same period.

| "Only 16 percent of those locked up in state prisons are there for drug crimes, and some of them probably belong there."

The War on Drugs Is Not to Blame for Mass Incarceration

Eli Hager and Bill Keller

In the following viewpoint Eli Hager and Bill Keller examine a book on the prison industrial complex by John Pfaff entitled Locked In. *The authors take points from Pfaff's book to address possible myths behind the standard narrative surrounding the prison industrial complex and emphasize data analysis and complexity. Eli Hager is a staff writer at the Marshall Project. Bill Keller is the founding editor in chief of the Marshall Project, a not-for-profit online journalism organization focusing on the criminal justice system in the US.*

As you read, consider the following questions:

1. How are John Pfaff's credentials "unusual"?
2. On what points does Pfaff agree with the general consensus on the prison industrial complex?
3. Why does a focus on drug arrests and convictions duck the question on how society should address violent crime?

"Everything You Think You Know About Mass Incarceration Is Wrong," by Eli Hager and Bill Keller, The Marshall Project, February 9, 2017. This article was originally published by the Marshall project, a non profit news organisation covering the US criminal justice system.

Critics of the prison-happy American criminal justice system tend to subscribe to a narrative that goes like this: Mass incarceration was ignited by the war on drugs (blame Nixon or Reagan), was pumped up by draconian sentencing and is now sustained by a "prison industrial complex" that puts profit before humane treatment and rehabilitation. John Pfaff, in his provocative new book, "Locked In," calls this the "Standard Story." And he challenges every element of that narrative.

Pfaff brings unusual credentials to the conversation. He is a law professor at Fordham University, but also a University of Chicago-trained economist, fluent in data analysis. He agrees with the pro-reform consensus that America's incarceration rate, which leads the world, is obscene and socially destructive. He also agrees that we could buy greater safety by investing instead in well-trained police and "noncustodial rehabilitation" such as drug treatment, mental health care and smart probation. But he invites us to rethink our notions about how we got to this state of affairs in the first place, in the hope that doing so will suggest some additional approaches to fixing things. "Most of the reform efforts today," he says, "are looking in the wrong places."

Here's what, in Pfaff's view, the "Standard Story" gets wrong.

The War on Drugs Is Not the Main Driver of Incarceration Rates That Have Grown Fivefold Since 1972

The most influential criminal justice book of this decade, Michelle Alexander's "The New Jim Crow," concluded that the war on drugs was central to the curse of mass incarceration. But in Pfaff's book, he contends the drug war is "important but unequivocally secondary to other factors." (One of those other factors was an actual rise in crime.) The numbers, he says, debunk the notion that prison populations can be drastically reduced by easing punishment for low-level drug offenses. Only 16 percent of those locked up in state prisons are there for drug crimes, and some of them probably belong there.

We exaggerate the role of drugs, Pfaff suspects, because we focus on federal prisons, where more than half of the inmate population is serving time for drugs. But federal prisons hold less than ten percent of the country's incarcerated.

Pfaff would still free many of those serving time for drugs, but he believes the focus on drug crimes ducks the more critical—and politically unpalatable—question of how we deal with violent crime. Some reformers have gone so far as to accept harsher minimum sentences for violent offenders as the price of cutting sentences for low-level drug offenders. (That was the gist of a proposed Senate compromise last year.) And since people convicted of violent crimes are the majority, that could mean no net reduction in overall incarceration rates in the long run.

Michelle Alexander, noting that she has not yet read Pfaff's book, said that such raw incarceration data misses her point about the war on drugs. "Some people get so caught up in the prison data...that they lose sight of the fact that the drug war was a game-changer culturally and politically," she said in an email. "The declaration and escalation of the War on Drugs marked a moment in our history when a group of people defined by race and class was defined as the 'enemy.' A literal war was declared on them, leading to a wave of punitiveness that affected every aspect of our criminal justice system...Counting heads in prisons and jails often obscures that social and political history. It also fails to grasp the significance of the drug war in mobilizing public opinion in support of harsh legislation and policies for all crimes. The drug war corrupted law enforcement by ramping up an 'us v. them' war mentality, transforming local police into domestic militaries... which wound up diverting energy, resources, and attention away from violent crime."

Pfaff says his differences with Alexander are "mostly semantic." He concurs with her that "the criminal justice system is driven by and exacerbates racial inequality."

Overly Long Sentences Are Not the Main Problem

Most of the criminal justice debate in Congress and at the state level has focused on rigid sentencing rules: mandatory minimum sentences, "truth in sentencing" laws that require offenders to serve at least 85 percent of their original sentence, "three strikes" laws that can send away repeat offenders for decades. It's true that criminal sentences in the US are much longer than international norms, and, on the books, they have gotten longer. But Pfaff calculates that—while the press has focused on some outrageous exceptions—the time actually served by Americans sent to prison has grown very little. Sentencing reform legislation that does away with mandatory minimum sentences for low-level crimes is, in other words, worth doing, but not game-changing.

The real problem, he says, is not "time served" but rather the sheer rate of admissions into prisons, which have skyrocketed since the 1980s. And that can only be fixed by reining in the day-to-day charging decisions of prosecutors (see below).

The For-Profit "Prison Industrial Complex" Is Not the Main Problem, Either

For all the attention paid to private prisons and the lobbying efforts of their corporate operators, they house only slightly more than seven percent of state prison inmates, and about 17 percent of the much smaller federal system. Twenty states, including New York and Illinois, have no private prisons at all. To be sure, for-profit companies also run prison cafeterias and health care operations, supply clothing, telephone services, and merchandise for prison commissaries, transport extradited prisoners and otherwise feed off of incarceration. But they are a small factor in driving growth, Pfaff says.

More important factors are powerful prison guard unions defending jobs and wages, and politicians who (usually incorrectly) see the local prison as an economic boon. "Yes, private firms have incentives to maximize the number of prisoners—but so do public sector actors, and they often have stronger incentives to do so, not to mention easier access to the politicians," Pfaff writes. "In fact, public prisons suffer from every pathology attributed to private prison firms. Every one, and likely in costlier ways."

Pfaff actually suggests that private prisons could be used to reduce incarceration. The trick is in writing better contracts, which have too often rewarded failure (when a former prisoner comes back, the private prison profits). "Imagine that instead of paying private prisons based on the number of prisoners they held each day, we paid them based on how those prisoners performed upon release," Pfaff says.

The Solution Is at the Front End, Not the Back End

Most reform efforts focus on getting people out of prison by shortening or abolishing minimum sentences, hastening the work of parole boards, awarding "earned time" for good behavior, and the like. Pfaff's most potent—and perhaps contentious—argument is that reforms should instead focus on bringing fewer felony charges against Americans in the first place. And that means zeroing in on prosecutors.

Pfaff's major data epiphany was that, during the 1990s and 2000s, as violent crime and arrests for violent crime both declined, the number of felony cases filed in state courts somehow went up. A lot. "In the end, the probability that a prosecutor would file felony charges against an arrestee basically doubled, and that change pushed prison populations up even as crime dropped," he writes.

Pfaff suggests several explanations for this. There were tens of thousands more prosecutors hired across the country in the 1990s and aughts even after the rising crime of the 1980s had stalled out, and the position of district attorney simultaneously became a more politically powerful one. Prosecutors' discretion, always great, was expanded by courts and legislatures. And public defenders, stuck at the same or lower levels of funding, have not kept up with the growing caseload.

Reformers have overlooked the role of prosecutors, Pfaff reasons, in part because there is no good data on how they use their discretion, and in part because they are simply less visible; about 95 percent of cases end in plea bargains worked out behind closed doors. "We see the police every day; no one is more high-profile in the criminal justice system," he said in an interview. "Then we think of the judge imposing the sentence." But prosecutors, and how they work, remain something of a mystery.

Pfaff's plea, then, is for advocates of reform to look for ways to curb the aggressiveness of prosecutors. He offers a tentative menu of options: establish guidelines for charging and plea bargaining, which New Jersey has already done; make prosecutors pay from their county budgets for the bed space they use in state prisons; and provide more funding for public defenders. And, last but not least, attack public complacency. In 46 states, prosecutors are elected—and 85 percent of them run without opposition. But last year, with money from philanthropist George Soros and energy from Black Lives Matter, insurgent district attorney candidates touting reform prevailed in several cities. And the American Civil Liberties Union has mapped out a three-year plan to increase public scrutiny of prosecutors."

I think that is already what the movement is shifting towards," said Udi Ofer, the ACLU's deputy political director, at a roundtable discussion of Pfaff's book this week. "John's book is just going to bolster that."

VIEWPOINT 3

> "Only a year into CCA's control
> of the facility, state audits found
> staff mismanagement, widespread
> violence, delays in medical treatment
> and unacceptable living conditions."

Prisons for Profit Is Immoral

Aubrie Bosworth

In the following viewpoint, Aubrie Bosworth focuses on one inmate incarcerated in a privately owned Montana prison. The author is specifically concerned with inmate human rights and has done extensive statistical research into the Corrections Corporation of America (CCA), the largest and oldest of the private prison companies now serving the prison industrial complex, in order to support her convictions. Aubrie Bosworth is a young journalist who wrote this viewpoint for Redoubt News, *a regional alternative online news and opinion publication.*

As you read, consider the following questions:

1. In which types of prisons is employee turnover higher?
2. Why does the author focus on Joe Robertson?
3. Why might excessively high employee turnover be an indication of problems within such a corporation?

Major concerns regarding Joe Robertson, 77 year old vet from Montana.

Is Mr. Robertson getting the care he needs? Is his life in danger? Here is my case against Corrections Corporation of America (CCA), who privately owns the prison in Montana in which Mr. Robertson is currently incarcerated.

CCA, founded in January 1983, is the nation's oldest and largest for-profit private prison corporation. Corrections Corporations of America manages more than 65 correctional and detention facilities with the capacity of more than 90,000 beds in 19 states and the District of Columbia.

A self-reported industry, statistics from 2000 showed that the average employee turnover rate was 53% in private prisons compared to the 15% employee turnover rate in public prisons. In 2008 Texas state reported that private prisons had a 90% annual staff turnover rate and public prisons had a 24%.

The first state prison sold to a private company is the Lake Erie Correctional Institution that was purchased by CCA from the state of Ohio in late 2011 for 72.7 million dollars. This transaction was deemed the groundbreaking move that will pave the way for fellow states seeking to cut costs. Only a year into CCA's control of the facility, state audits found staff mismanagement, widespread violence, delays in medical treatment and unacceptable living conditions. The audit detailed how staff did not follow proper procedures for chronically ill prisoners, including those with diabetes and AIDS, medical appointments were severely delayed, and prisoners were often triple-bunked or forced to sleep on mattresses on cell floors. As a result of the violations, CCA was fined nearly $500,000 by the state.

A Negligence in Training/ Employees Put in Danger

On August 5th, 1998 at Tennessee's Whiteville Correctional Facility a guard named Jerry Reeves was left alone on a recreation yard only six weeks into the job. He had no significant training or any communications equipment resulting in Reeves being seriously assaulted by prisoners. The assault left him with multiple skull fractures.

According to an article published by the Grassroots Leadership, on October 1st, 2009 CCA paid 1.3 million dollars to settle allegations of serious sexual harassment involving female employees at the company's Crowley Country Correctional Facility (CCCF) in Colorado. In a lawsuit filed by the US Equal Employment Opportunity Commission alleged that female staff was subjected to sexual abuse and rape at the facility, at times under the threat of losing their job. In one incident the court heard that CCA management reassigned a female officer to an isolated location of the facility with a male co-worker whom she had previously complained had sexually harassed her, when she was reassigned, the same man then raped her.

Violence Incited by CCA

Idaho Correctional Center (ICC) has a reputation of being one of the most violent correctional facilities in the US. With ICC's constant outbreaks of violence that is often watched and sometimes even incited by CCA guards ICC has picked up the nickname "Gladiator School."

An attorney for an inmate that was held at Gladiator School finally got through to the media for his client to blow the whistle on the violence that was going on inside ICC. Later after this inmate served his time and was released his body was found in his pickup in the middle of the East Fork and South Fork of the Salmon River near Yellow Pine, his death was ruled an accident.

In 2012 Boise law firm sued CCA on behalf of inmates within ICC. The inmates claimed that CCA had taken control over the gangs inside of the Gladiator School and was using the gangs so they could under-staff the prison so CCA could cut back on employee wages.

The press discovered CCA had charged the state for nonexistent guards for about $12 million in a single year. The press didn't receive records for the other years. CCA's contract with the state

"The Worst Prison in the Country"

Biography is something we associate with "great figures" of history: generals, politicians, writers, artists and reformers. Rarely is the form used for an institution, particularly one which housed many people on the edge of society. *Mansions of Misery* cleverly weaves individual tales of impoverishment into the general tapestry of London life in the 18th and early 19th centuries. Some chapters focus on the debtor experiences of notable inmates, such as the musician John Grano, who inhabited the Marshalsea in the 1720s, and Charles Dickens' own father John, who served a spell almost 100 years later. This paints a clear picture of how the Marshalsea evolved over time and the different types of people who came into contact with "the worst prison in the country." Included in these fascinating vignettes are the optician Joshua Reeve Lowe, who had saved Queen Victoria from assassination, and the noted swindler James Stamp Sutton Cooke.

The real strength of this book is undoubtedly the way the author brings to life the daily struggles of the debtor's world, as well as the often questionable actions of those enforcing the rule of law. Anecdotal accounts, such as bailiffs trying to arrest the body of a deceased debtor, are plentiful, as well as examples of unscrupulous creditors abusing "mesne process" to arrest debtors, some as young as four, without having to prove it in court. There is a comprehensive analysis of the ruthless ways in which everyone from simple turnkeys, charged with the day to day running of the prison, to notorious deputy marshals, such as William Acton, "skinned the flint" in order to exploit the inmates for profit. The work is very even-handed, with plenty of instances of right and wrong on both sides of the economic divide.

The prison itself is richly described in detail, cleverly depicted as a microcosm of society: from the Common side, where the poor were housed, to the Master's side, for those of greater means such as Grano, who often survived on aid from long-suffering friends and family. There was a surprisingly large range of amenities on site, including an alehouse, coffee shop, chandlery, chapel and space and equipment for sports and recreations. *Mansions of Misery* is altogether a well-paced and informative work that deals with a weighty subject in an objective and stimulating way.

"Marshalsea: The Worst Prison in the Country," by Jerry White, History Today Ltd, June 2017.

of Idaho was worth about $29 million a year, the company agreed to pay $1 million to settle the under-staffing claims.

So not a good track record for CCA. It is clear that they cut many corners to save a bit of money. Money that they enjoy at the expense of their employees and as we look into the well being of the prisoners it's not any prettier.

Gross Denial of Medical Care

September 2006 at Arizona's Eloy Detention Center Jose Lopez-Gregario committed suicide. Jose was on suicide watch, and was known to be despondent and had made medical requests to CCA staff who failed to respond.

In 1988 CCA was accused of failing to provide adequate medical care and a lawsuit was filed by the family of twenty-three year old Rosalind Bradford who was being held at CCA's Silverdale Facility in Tennessee. Rosalind died from pregnancy complications. A shift supervisor testified that Rosalind was in extreme pain for at least 12 hours before staff agreed to have her transported to the hospital. CCA agreed to pay $100,000 to settle the lawsuit.

A lawsuit was filed against CCA in 2004 over the death of 27 year old quadriplegic Jonathan Magbie who was held at Correctional Treatment Center in DC. Jonathan was not given his diaphragmatic ventilator which led to him dying of respiratory failure four days into a ten day sentence.

These are just a very small handful of the lawsuits and allegations against CCA.

I long to question our founding fathers, is privately owned prisons that a profit is being made from even constitutional? I will say that at least it is definitely immoral.

Mr. Robertson

Joe Robertson is a 77 year old veteran who was put in prison for building a pond on his private property. Joe using someone else's calling cards was able to have a one 30-60 second phone call with his wife. Where he informed her that he was not well. He continues to have chest pain and the prison refuses to give him his regular medication. Mr. Robertson should have a minimum of $50 that would have been transferred from Missoula county, and yet he still has to use someone else's calling cards.

No one is able to send money yet because anyone including his wife must be on a pre-approved list and has to go through a complete background check for visitation with Mr. Robertson before the prison will accept any funds for his commissary. Joe's heath continues to worsen, he recently had a stroke and was taken to the hospital for a few test but was then forced back to his cell. He is having trouble seeing and can barely walk half way around the yard compared to the 6-7 laps he would usually make when he was allowed out of his cell. He is now forced to stay in his cell because the staff "fears" of him falling.

Will Robertson's Case Be Like Jeffery Buller's?

Twenty-six year old Jeffery Buller died one day before he was to be released causing his mother to file a lawsuit against CCA in March of 2003. Jeffery was being held at Colorado's Kit Carson Correctional Center. He suffered from Hereditary Angioedema, which caused his breathing passages to swell. This could be easily and effectively be controlled with medication. Throughout Jeffery's incarceration he had been supplied with medication but the last few weeks of his stay the supply ran out. Despite his repeated pleas for a new prescription with CCA's medical staff no new supply was reordered. CCA settled the lawsuit out of court in 2004.

I beg to question Corrections Corporations of America, is this just ongoing abuse in privately owned prisons or is this deliberate medical neglect of Joe Robertson?

How much longer do the corrupted elite expect us to keep submitting ourselves to this perverted justice system?

What recourse do we have left?

Do we go and appeal to another tyrannical judge?

Appeal to another level of tyranny higher up the chain hoping that we might win and walk away with our life and liberties still intact?

Do we keep submitting ourselves to this tyrannical justice systems which convict citizens of felonies, not based on laws enacted by their elected legislature's, but for violations of department policies put in place by UN-elected bureaucrats thousands of miles from the real world in which American citizens live?

When do we draw the line and stop putting our liberties and lives into their already blood-stained hands?

Nevada Assemblywoman Michele Fiore says in a video:

My message to you is we can change things, we've become an effete society which means weak, spoiled, lazy and no longer able to take effective action. I'm here sending you this message because you can take effective action.

"*Today, however, the situation has reversed itself: now people do care about mass incarceration, largely thanks to the Black Lives Matter movement and the intense scrutiny it has focused on police killings.*"

A 1994 Crime Bill Destroyed Lives

Thomas Frank

In the following viewpoint, Thomas Frank argues that former president Bill Clinton is largely responsible for the rapid increase in mass incarceration rates in the United States. Clinton's administration passed crime legislation in 1994 that was especially detrimental for low-level drug offenses among people of color and has adversely affected the African American community. The author offers that it is particularly rich that Clinton had criticized mass incarceration just weeks before signing the bill. Thomas Frank is a political and cultural analyst who has written several noted books including What's the Matter with Kansas? *(2004) and* Listen, Liberal *(2016).*

"Bill Clinton's Crime Bill Destroyed Lives, and There's No Point Denying It," by Thomas Frank, Guardian News and Media Limited, April 15, 2016. Reprinted by permission.

As you read, consider the following questions:

1. What specifically is the author criticizing former president Bill Clinton for?
2. What pro-incarceration slogans was the 1994 crime bill known for?
3. How does the fact that this viewpoint was written on the eve of the 2016 US presidential election affect the tone of the message?

Here is an actual headline that appeared in the *New York Times* this week: Prison Rate Was Rising Years Before 1994 Law.

It is an unusual departure for a newspaper, since what is being reported here is not news but history—or, rather, a particular interpretation of history. The "1994 Law" to which the headline refers is the Violent Crime Control and Law Enforcement Act; the statement about the "prison rate" refers to the fact that America was already imprisoning a large portion of its population before that 1994 law was approved by Congress.

As historical interpretations go, this one is pretty non-controversial. Everyone who has heard about the "War on Drugs" knows that what we now call "mass incarceration," the de facto national policy of locking up millions of low-level offenders, began long before 1994. And yet similar stories reporting that non-startling fact are now being published all across the American media landscape. That mass incarceration commenced before 1994 is apparently Big News.

Why report a historical fact that everyone already knows? The answer is because former president Bill Clinton, the man who called for and signed the 1994 crime bill, is also the husband of the current frontrunner for the Democratic presidential nomination, and Democratic voters are having trouble squaring his draconian crime bill with his wife's liberal image.

That might be the reason so many of these stories seem to unfold with the same goal in mind: to minimize Clinton's moral culpability for what went on back in the 1990s. Mass incarceration was already happening, these stories agree. And besides, not everything in the crime bill was bad. As for its lamentable effects, well, they weren't intentional. What's more, Bill Clinton has apologized for it. He's sorry for all those thousands of people who have had decades of their lives ruined by zealous prosecutors and local politicians using the tools Clinton accidentally gave them. He sure didn't mean for that to happen.

When I was researching the 1994 crime bill for *Listen, Liberal*, my new book documenting the sins of liberalism, I remember being warned by a scholar who has studied mass incarceration for years that it was fruitless to ask Americans to care about the thousands of lives destroyed by the prison system. Today, however, the situation has reversed itself: now people do care about mass incarceration, largely thanks to the Black Lives Matter movement and the intense scrutiny it has focused on police killings.

All of a sudden, the punitive frenzies of the 1980s and 1990s seem like something from a cruel foreign country. All of a sudden, Bill Clinton looks like a monster rather than a hero, and he now finds himself dogged by protesters as he campaigns for his wife, Hillary. And so the media has stepped up to do what it always does: reassure Americans that the nightmare isn't real, that this honorable man did the best he could as president.

Allow me to offer a slightly different take on the 1990s. I think today (as I thought at the time) that there is indeed something worth criticizing when a Democratic president signs on to a national frenzy for punishment and endorses things like "three strikes," "mandatory minimums," and "truth in sentencing," the latter being a cute euphemism for "no more parole." The reason the 1994 crime bill upsets people is not because they stupidly believe Bill Clinton invented these things; it is because they know he encouraged them. Because the Democrats' capitulation to the rightwing incarceration agenda was a turning point in its own right.

Another interesting fact. Two weeks after Clinton signed the big crime bill in September 1994, he enacted the Riegle-Neal interstate banking bill, the first in a series of moves deregulating the financial industry. The juxtaposition between the two is kind of shocking, when you think about it: low-level drug users felt the full weight of state power at the same moment that bankers saw the shackles that bound them removed. The newspaper headline announcing the discovery of this amazing historical finding will have to come from my imagination—Back-to-Back 1994 Laws Freed Bankers And Imprisoned Poor, perhaps—but the historical pattern is worth noting nevertheless, since it persisted all throughout Clinton's administration.

For one class of Americans, Clinton brought emancipation, a prayed-for deliverance from out of Glass–Steagall's house of bondage. For another class of Americans, Clinton brought discipline: long prison stretches for drug users; perpetual insecurity for welfare mothers; and intimidation for blue-collar workers whose bosses Clinton thoughtfully armed with the North American Free Trade Agreement. As I have written elsewhere, some got the carrot, others got the stick.

But what is most shocking in our current journo-historical understanding of the Clinton years is the idea that the mass imprisonment of people of color was an "unintended consequence" of the 1994 crime bill, to quote the *New York Daily News*'s paraphrase of Hillary Clinton. This is flatly, glaringly false, as the final, ugly chapter of the crime bill story confirms.

Back in the early 1990s, and although they were chemically almost identical, crack and powder cocaine were regarded very differently by the law. The drug identified with black users (crack) was treated as though it were 100 times as villainous as the same amount of cocaine, a drug popular with affluent professionals. This "now-notorious 100-to-one" sentencing disparity, as the *New York Times* put it, had been enacted back in 1986, and the 1994 crime law instructed the US Sentencing Commission to study the subject and adjust federal sentencing guidelines as it saw fit.

The Sentencing Commission duly recommended that the 100-to-1 sentencing disparity be abolished, largely because (as their lengthy report on the subject put it) "The 100-to-1 crack cocaine to powder cocaine quantity ratio is a primary cause of the growing disparity between sentences for black and white federal defendants." By the time their report was released, however, Republicans had gained control of Congress, and they passed a bill explicitly overturning the decision of the Sentencing Commission. (Bernie Sanders, for the record, voted against that bill.)

The bill then went to President Clinton for approval. Shortly before it came to his desk he gave an inspiring speech deploring the mass incarceration of black Americans. "Blacks are right to think something is terribly wrong," he said on that occasion, "… when there are more African American men in our correction system than in our colleges; when almost one in three African American men, in their twenties, are either in jail, on parole, or otherwise under the supervision of the criminal system. Nearly one in three."

Two weeks after that speech, however, Clinton blandly affixed his signature to the bill retaining the 100-to-1 sentencing disparity, a disparity that had brought about the lopsided incarceration of black people. Clinton could have vetoed it, but he didn't. He signed it.

Today we are told that mass incarceration was an "unintended consequence" of Clinton's deeds.

For that to be true, however, Clinton would have not only had to ignore the Sentencing Commission's findings but also to ignore the newspaper stories appearing all around him, which can be found easily on the internet to this day. Here's one that appeared in the Baltimore Sun on 31 October 1995, in which it is noted that:

> Civil rights organizations had led a telephone campaign to pressure the president to veto the bill. At a rally last week in Chicago, the Rev Jesse L Jackson said that Mr Clinton had the chance, "with one stroke of your veto pen, to correct the most grievous racial injustice built into our legal system."

It is impossible to imagine that Bill Clinton, the brilliant Rhodes Scholar, didn't understand what everyone was saying. How could he sign such a thing right after giving a big speech deploring its effects? How can he and his wife now claim it was all an accident, when the consequences were being discussed everywhere at the time? When everyone was warning and even begging him not to do it? Maybe it didn't really happen. Maybe it was all a bad dream.

But it did happen. There it is, Bill Clinton's signing statement on the website of the American Presidency Project. Yes, the 100-to-1 disparity was finally reduced in 2010, but we liberals still can't ignore what Clinton did back in 1995. Every historian who writes about his administration will eventually have to deal with it.

Until then, we have our orders from the mainstream media: Clinton didn't mean it. Clinton has apologized. Things were bad even before Clinton got started.

It is a hell of a way to do history. Millions of proudly open-minded people are being asked to twist themselves into propaganda pretzels to avoid acknowledging the obvious: that the leaders of our putatively left party aren't who we think they are.

Periodical and Internet Sources Bibliography

The following articles have been selected to supplement the diverse views presented in this chapter.

Matt Bump, "The War on Drugs, Part II. The Prison Industrial Complex," Medium.com, January 2019, https://medium .com/@mattbump_57520/the-war-on-drugs-part-ii-the-prison -industrial-complex-be19dd7b6809.

Ed Chung, Betsy Pearl, and Lea Hunter, "The 1994 Crime Bill Continues to Undercut Justice Reform—Here's How to Stop It," American Progress, March 26, 2019, https://www .americanprogress.org/issues/criminal-justice /reports/2019/03/26/467486/1994-crime-bill-continues -undercut-justice-reform-heres-stop/.

Ruth Wilson Gilmore and James Kilgore, "Some Reflections on Prison Labor," The Brooklyn Rail, June 2019, https://brooklynrail .org/2019/06/field-notes/Some-Reflections-on-Prison-Labor.

Eli Hager and Bill Keller, "Everything You Think You Know About Mass Incarceration Is Wrong," The Marshall Project, February 9, 2017, https://www.themarshallproject.org/2017/02/09 /everything-you-think-you-know-about-mass-incarceration -is-wrong.

Jessica Lussenhop, "Clinton Crime Bill: Why Is It so Controversial?" BBC, April 18, 2016, https://www.bbc.com/news/world-us -canada-36020717.

Madison Pauly, "A Brief History of America's Private Prison Industry," Mother Jones, July 2016, https://www.motherjones.com /politics/2016/06/history-of-americas-private-prison-industry -timeline/.

John Derek Stern, "The War on Drugs and Jim Crow's the Most Wanted: A Social and Historical Look at Mass Incarceration," *Ramapo Journal of Law & Society*, June 15, 2017, https://www .ramapo.edu/law-journal/thesis/war-drugs-jim-crows-wanted -social-historical-look-mass-incarceration/.

OPPOSING
VIEWPOINTS®
SERIES

CHAPTER 3

What Are the Economic and Social Implications of the Prison Industrial Complex?

Chapter Preface

The prison industrial complex isn't just a set of private prisons. It is also an economic and social driver enmeshed in the American way of life, essentially touching every aspect of our society, in both private and public sectors. Eric Schlosser defines it as "a set of bureaucratic, political, and economic interests that encourage increased spending on imprisonment, regardless of the actual need."

One of the most important things that can be said about the prison industrial complex is that it is an abstract concept that has real life consequences affecting everyday people. The prison industrial complex effectively removes "unexploitable" labor, the so-called underclass Americans from society and re-creates them as a highly exploitable cheap labor force many large companies use to dominate our economy.

There are approximately 400,000 immigrants detained every year in the United States, and 50 percent of those are housed in private prison complexes. Additionally, over half of the private prison corporation's income comes from immigrant detention activities.

The following chapter includes a diverse range of viewpoints at the cross-section of the economic/social prism. Viewpoints examine how nearly all of the major US banks were once invested in the private prison industry (although now under activist pressure, many are divesting their interests). They explore the idea that the PIC is fully exploiting low-income people and people of color for profit and for labor. They focus on how young people's lives are derailed by the so-called school-to-prison pipeline, how the mentally ill population has been shuffled along the system into prisons instead of being offered treatment, and how immigrants are being held in the world's largest detention system, a significant part of the US economy.

> *"As Trump has escalated his anti-immigrant policies, the prison divestment movement has become a broad coalition, connecting immigrant rights groups with the movement to end mass incarceration in the United States."*

Under Pressure from Activists, Big Banks Are Divesting from Private Prisons

Mike Ludwig

In the following viewpoint Mike Ludwig details how large banks currently invested in the private prison industry are being forced, through mass public outrage and activist efforts, to end private financing of corporate prison firms. Mike Ludwig is a staff reporter at Truthout, covering independent news stories that the corporate media outlets tend to ignore.

As you read, consider the following questions:

1. How did the Trump administration's actions affect the decisions of major banks to divest from privatized prisons?
2. Which large banks in particular does the author name?
3. What commitment does the author conclude is needed for the future to end mass incarceration?

"Big Banks Are Divesting from Private Prisons, Thanks to Anti-ICE Activism," by Mike Ludwig, Truthout, July 23, 2019. https://truthout.org/articles/big-banks-are-divesting-from-private-prisons-thanks-to-anti-ice-activism/. Reprinted by permission.

M ajor private prison firms CoreCivic and GEO Group stand to lose 72 percent—about $1.9 billion—of their private financing as major banks commit to divesting from the private prison industry under pressure from activists, according to a new analysis by the Center for Popular Democracy and other groups.

Activists have been pushing banks, pension funds, colleges, and city and state governments to divest from the private prison industry for years. However, the movement's momentum has recently grown: Public outrage over Trump administration policies at the southern border has put mounting pressure on Wall Street to drop financial support for private companies that contract with Immigration and Customs Enforcement (ICE) to service and run a vast network of immigration jails and detention centers.

The National Immigrant Justice Center reports that about 71 percent of people in ICE custody were held at private facilities in 2017, although that number may be higher now that the Trump administration's punitive border policies have caused populations of incarcerated migrants and asylum seekers to swell in notoriously overcrowded jails and detention pens. CoreCivic and GEO Group, the nation's two largest private prison firms, are among ICE's top private contractors for incarcerating and transporting immigrants. (In contrast, only 8.5 percent of state and federal prisoners are held in private jails and prisons.)

Private prison firms profit from human suffering and are known to cut corners in order to save money, practices that have created a long list of controversies at immigration jails as well as state and federal prisons, including lawsuits alleging labor trafficking of immigration detainees. Private prison firms are also beholden to investors and financiers, creating an array of public targets for activists.

As Trump has escalated his anti-immigrant policies, the prison divestment movement has become a broad coalition, connecting immigrant rights groups with the movement to end mass incarceration in the United States, which has long been driven by activists working at the intersection of human rights and racial justice. Kristin Rowe-Finkbeiner, executive director of the progressive action network MomsRising and a member of the Families Belong Together Corporate Accountability Committee, said more than 100 grassroots groups came together over the past few months to put pressure on the banks with petitions, protests and sit-ins, building on years of organizing by prison divestment activists.

"What we're seeing is a wave of mass outrage being turned into a wave of mass action, and we're seeing people discovering that they have power to make corporate change and legislative change and cultural change to change the narrative," Rowe-Finkbeiner said in an interview with *Truthout*.

So far this year, six major banks—JPMorgan Chase, Wells Fargo, Bank of America, SunTrust, BNP Paribas, and Fifth Third Bancorp—have made broad public commitments to no longer provide new financing to the private prison industry after current financial agreements expire. This divestment is expected to have a considerable impact on GEO Group and CoreCivic, which rely on loans and lines of credit to expand and stay afloat.

Both companies are set up as Real Estate Investment Trusts (REITs) that are exempt from corporate income taxes, an arrangement that has allowed the private prison industry to expand rapidly over the past two decades. However, REITs are required by law to pass large portions of their incomes back to investors, limiting the amount of cash they have on hand. So, in order to expand their operations while sustaining the business model based on the REIT tax loophole, companies like CoreCivic and GEO Group must rely on short-term loans and lines of credit, making Wall Street financing for private prison firms a crucial choke point of activists.

"Wall Street severing ties with private prisons doesn't just tarnish the public reputation of these companies," said Maggie Corser, a Center for Popular Democracy analyst, in a statement. "It stands to materially hurt the bottom line of for-profit prison companies for years to come."

Several banks facing pressure to divest from private prison companies, including PNC Bank, Barclays and US Bank, have not committed publicly to divesting, according to the Center's analysis. Moreover, those that have publicly said they would no longer finance private prison firms are not keeping their commitments equally. For example, Wells Fargo and JPMorgan Chase have already canceled credit lines for GEO Group, while Bank of America extended an additional $90 million revolving credit line to the company shortly before announcing that it would no longer offer new financing to the industry.

It's also unclear what portions of the sprawling private prison industry the banks will no longer finance. Bank of America officials made its divestment announcement after touring the Homestead center, a privately run migrant "influx center" in Miami that human rights groups say is really a detention center where children are held for long periods of time in grueling conditions and are unable to leave. Caliburn, the private company behind Homestead, does not expect to be impacted by Bank of America's decision because it is not technically a private prison, according to reports.

GEO Group has also attempted to distance itself from the controversies surrounding the separation of families and detention of migrant children, telling media outlets that it does not manage facilities that house unaccompanied minors or those under control of the Border Patrol.

Even if the banks were to divest entirely from companies that run private prisons, that wouldn't necessarily mean no more profiting from incarceration. The nation's sprawling system of incarceration is full of for-profit companies, including within public prisons: Contractors may provide everything from medical care to food and phone calls home.

Moreover, as Truthout's Kelly Hayes recently pointed out, the core problem is not that children are being caged in privately run detention facilities. The problem is that children are being caged at all, thanks to the criminalization of people of all ages for migrating. Migrants are swept into the country's system of mass incarceration, which disproportionately cages people of color, whether they are immigrants or not.

"On the one end, seeing immigrant detention as an extension of mass incarceration is super important … it's not just a Latino issue, but a Black issue, and also an issue impacting other communities as well," said Daniel Carrillo, executive director of Freedom to Thrive, a racial justice group with a longstanding prison divestment campaign. "It's part of a bigger system that is divesting resources from communities and pushing those resources into prisons and detention, so we should be thinking about how we should reallocate and push for reinvestment and demand that from private and public actors."

Carrillo said activists should make demands beyond divestment from prison profiteers and remember that it's not enough to simply call for an ICE or Border Patrol detention facility to be shut down. GEO Group and other companies are heavily invested in "alternatives" to incarceration like ankle monitors and facial recognition technology that can extend the system of control and incarceration beyond the walls of a jail or detention center.

"The profit motive continues and the motive of control of communities continues as well," Carrillo said.

The prison divestment movement has certainly benefited from the outrage over the mass incarceration of immigrants, and if financial institutions stick to their commitments, the private prison industry could face big problems in the long run. This will not put an end to mass incarceration in this country, or the abuse that migrants face under the Trump administration. Legislation and systemic shifts in the legal system are needed for that. But it is proof that activists can hold financial institutions accountable for investing in human rights abuses, and those who profit from misery can be hit where it hurts—in the wallet.

> *"Mass incarceration, which
> disproportionately impacts poor
> people of color, has exacerbated
> and further racialized the problems
> of mental illness. It is both cause
> and effect. Cycling in and out of
> prisons and jails is traumatic, often
> undermining prospects for economic
> and social stability."*

The Intersection Between Race, Mental Illness, and Incarceration Must Be Closely Analyzed

James Kilgore

In the following viewpoint, James Kilgore argues that for too long jail has been the solution for police dealing with public situations involving the mentally ill. This is because the number of public mental health institutions has dwindled, resulting in the criminality of mental illness. When the factors of race and social class are added, we get a vicious cycle of incarceration, lack of mental health treatment, and poverty. James Kilgore is an activist, writer, and researcher based in Urbana, Illinois. He is the director of the Challenging E-Carceration project, which focuses on developing critical responses to electronic monitoring and other carceral technologies.

As you read, consider the following questions:

1. What does the author mean when he writes the work achieved by Dorothea Dix now stands as ancient history?
2. How are poverty and mental illness connected, according to the viewpoint?
3. Why is there fear of shifting from a prison industrial complex to a treatment industrial complex?

In 1843, social justice crusader Dorothea Dix went before the Massachusetts Legislature with the intention of addressing an acute problem of the day: the incarceration of people with mental illness. Her declaration to the assembly highlighted the "state of Insane Persons," protesting that they were confined "in cages, stalls, pens! Chained, naked, beaten with rods, and lashed into obedience." Her efforts led to the creation of the state's first mental health hospitals. For the next several years, Dix travelled from state to state, repeating her cycle of advocating for special facilities for people living with mental illness apart from jails and prisons. Though she was successful in many states, her work now stands as ancient history. When it comes to mental health, we have retreated back to the days of the "cages, stalls and pens."

In many communities, jails have become the only option for police confronted with a person in mental health crisis in public. The reason behind this is obvious: the virtual shutdown of the nation's public mental health care system for which Dix fought. From 1970 to 2002, the per capita number of public mental health hospital beds plummeted from 207 per 100,000 to 20 per 100,000. The intent of these closures was to dismantle large, often punitive mental institutions and replace them with community-based facilities that would have a more patient-centered ethos. Unfortunately, these closures took place at a moment when neoliberalism was on the rise. In the name of fiscal responsibility, most states simply did not replace mental health institutions. In many instances, jails became the quick fix to handle poor people who had mental health crises and no access to treatment.

By 2004, a Department of Justice survey found that 64 percent of local jail populations and 56 percent of those in prisons had symptoms of mental illness. More recent studies cited in a 2014 report by the National Research Council show no abatement of this situation. The presence of mental illness among incarcerated women is particularly acute. A 2009 survey of Maryland and New York jails showed that 31 percent of women had serious mental illnesses, more than double the rate for men.

Though no Dorothea Dix figure has emerged in 2015, at long last policy makers and researchers are waking up to the issue. More than 50 counties, including Champaign, Illinois, where I live, have passed a resolution circulated by the Council on State Governments, backing treatment in the community rather than incarceration. This resolution, part of an initiative called "Stepping Up," comes on the heels of major research reports by Human Rights Watch and the Urban Institute on the challenges of mental illness in jails and prisons.

While attention to this problem is long overdue, the framing of Stepping Up as well as the work by Human Rights Watch and the Urban Institute suffers from a common but crucial blind spot: no mention of race. As Michelle Alexander and others have tirelessly pointed out, racism pervades the prison industrial complex. No serious attempt at reform, let alone transformation, can ignore this.

Overlooked Issues of Race

In the intersection between mental health and incarceration, at least four racial issues surface. First, the petition and recent reports present a static model of the relationship between mental health and incarceration. The assumed dynamic holds that people have pre-existing mental health issues, which get misinterpreted as criminality, resulting in arrest and lockup. The cure then becomes putting people into treatment rather than behind bars.

While choosing treatment over incarceration may represent a step forward, policy makers and practitioners need to dig deeper into the complex root causes of mental illness. Often, treatment is far from enough. Mental illness can be the product of individual circumstances—a traumatic event, a person's brain chemistry or even their genetic makeup. However, a considerable body of research links many instances of mental illness to experiences of poverty and violence, which are disproportionate realities in poor communities of color.

Researcher Jack Carney outlines the relationship between poverty and mental illness in his provocatively titled article, "Poverty and Mental Illness: You Can't Have One Without The Other." Indeed, the violence of poverty can often trigger poor mental health. People may have mental illness because they have grown up without sufficient nutrition or without access to adequate education, housing or career opportunities. Mental illness may also be precipitated by an environment where fear of racialized police violence, deportation or domestic abuse is a constant reality.

These are structural problems which medication, therapy groups or wraparound services cannot reverse. As "Elizabeth," a homeless Massachusetts woman with a history of mental health problems, told Susan Sered, a Suffolk University professor, "I don't need to talk about my problems. I need a place to live so that I won't be scared all of the time."

The Trauma of Incarceration

Secondly, mass incarceration, which disproportionately impacts poor people of color, has exacerbated and further racialized the problems of mental illness. It is both cause and effect. Cycling in and out of prisons and jails is traumatic, often undermining prospects for economic and social stability. Long-term incarceration, especially in high security or supermax facilities, accentuates the problem. All of this has worsened due to the cutbacks in education and job training programs in prison in the last three decades, heightening the possibility of depression while incarcerated and lack of opportunity after release.

In addition, offering quality mental health treatment in prisons and jails can be difficult. On the one hand, as psychology professor Craig Haney has noted, "prisoners are reluctant to open up in environments where they do not feel physically or psychologically safe." On the other, institutional realities—violence, poor food, lockdowns, isolation and racial discrimination—further inhibit progress for mental health patients. As James Pleasant, currently finishing his 13th year of incarceration in Minnesota, said, "Sleeping on a concrete slab will not solve mental health issues."

Even if treatment is effective, Haney argues that the transition to care outside of prisons is frequently "spotty" because there's not an effective pass-off to the service providers in the community. Some war veterans and survivors of violent attacks may qualify for PTSD therapy, but such services are rarely available to those suffering from post-incarceration stress. They are left to cope for themselves, generally with very few resources.

Racial Stereotyping and a Lack of Cultural Competency

A third key issue is racial stereotyping. This takes several forms. At the level of day-to-day police responses, Dr. Tiffany Townsend, a senior director in the American Psychological Association's Public Interest Directorate, has stressed that Black people are "more likely to be ushered into the criminal justice system" as opposed to being placed in treatment. In other cases, stereotyping can have even more serious consequences. The cases of Ezell Ford in Los Angeles, Lavall Hall in Miami Gardens and Michelle Cusseaux in Phoenix, all killed by police, constitute evidence that Black individuals in mental health crises run serious risks of being criminalized and "treated" with fatal gunfire rather than de-escalation or crisis intervention techniques.

Lastly, mental health treatment, both within carceral institutions and beyond, reflects the greater racial politics of society at large.

From the days of diagnosing runaway enslaved people with an affliction called drapetomania in the 1800s to the labeling of Black protesters in the 1960s as schizophrenic, the mental health establishment has a considerable legacy of racist practice.

This history still impacts the attitudes of both mental health practitioners and patients. In 1999, a surgeon general's report noted the inferiority of mental health services provided to people of color. A 2014 research team from Morehouse College of Medicine showed that the problems persist. Such disparities are reinforced by the lack of people of color, especially African Americans, among mental health care professionals. According to a recent article posted by the National Alliance on Mental Illness, Black people make up just 3.7 percent of members in the American Psychiatric Association and 1.5 percent of those in the American Psychological Association.

Black psychologist Dr. Josephine Johnson argues that "cultural competency," which the National Institutes of Health define as "the ability to deliver services that are respectful of and responsive to the health beliefs, practices and cultural and linguistic needs of diverse patients," is an "ethical mandate." Cultural competency of care providers for those who have had involvement with the criminal legal system may be especially critical for those who have had negative experiences with white authority figures along the street-to-prison pipeline.

The lack of cultural competency appears in the carceral setting as well. In an interview with Truthout, Melissa Thompson, a professor at Portland State University, said that in researching her book *Mad or Bad? Race, Class, Gender, and Mental Disorder in the Criminal Justice System*, she found racial disparities between Black people and white people "quite pervasive." She carried out both in an intensive study of Hennepin County Jail in Minnesota and a review of national data. She cited racial differences in regard to mental health relating to how people were charged, their access to and quality of treatment received in prisons and jails as well as conditions of probation and parole. These differences even remained when she "confined her analysis to those who self-identified as mentally ill."

Mental Health Support or Medical Control?

Finally, even if present efforts in carceral mental health do develop a racial consciousness, it may not be enough. Some researchers fear we may be shifting from one punishment paradigm to another, as some people describe it, from a prison industrial complex to a "treatment-industrial complex."

Sociologist Susan Sered expressed the concern to Truthout that the transition from "criminal" to "mentally ill" points to a change in status from "someone who did something bad and can serve his or her debt to society" to "someone who is fundamentally and permanently sick."

In her view, an uncaring or poorly conceptualized mental health "alternative" could end up looking much more like medical control and even experimentation rather than a genuine transformation of public policy and invigoration of the communities that have been devastated by mass incarceration and criminalization of their populations.

Hence, while the call for reducing the population of people living with mentall illness in jails is timely and necessary, advocates of mental health decarceration need to embrace a more nuanced analysis of the intersection between race, mental illness and incarceration. Without this, little substantive change is likely to result.

> *"Having a zero tolerance policy means that a school has zero tolerance for any kind of misbehavior or violation of school rules, no matter how minor, unintentional, or subjectively defined it may be."*

The School-to-Prison Pipeline Has Caused Great Harm to Communities of Color

Nicki Lisa Cole, PhD

In the following viewpoint Nicki Lisa Cole argues that the school-to-prison pipeline is fueled by racial bias and as a result inflicts lasting damage on black and Latino families and communities. The school-to-prison-pipeline can be defined as a set of specific policies, such as harsh school rules and zero tolerance municipal laws, that increasingly see minors and young adults from disadvantaged backgrounds incarcerated. Nicki Lisa Cole is a researcher at the Stockholm Environment Institute and in Social Policy at the University of York. Her areas of research include corporate power and its implications, and consumer culture, ethics, and behavior.

"Understanding the School-to-Prison Pipeline," by Nicki Lisa Cole, PhD. Dotdash publishing, May 30, 2019. Reprinted by permission.

As you read, consider the following questions:

1. What does the author list as the main reasons the school-to-prison pipeline now has a foothold in American schools?
2. Why might the school-to-prison pipeline especially affect black students?
3. What is labeling theory and how does it apply here?

The school-to-prison pipeline is a process through which students are pushed out of schools and into prisons. In other words, it is a process of criminalizing youth that is carried out by disciplinary policies and practices within schools that put students into contact with law enforcement. Once they are put into contact with law enforcement for disciplinary reasons, many are then pushed out of the educational environment and into the juvenile and criminal justice systems.

The key policies and practices that created and now maintain the school-to-prison pipeline include zero tolerance policies that mandate harsh punishments for both minor and major infractions, exclusion of students from schools through punitive suspensions and expulsions, and the presence of police on campus as School Resource Officers (SROs).

The school-to-prison pipeline is supported by budgetary decisions made by the US government. From 1987-2007, funding for incarceration more than doubled while funding for higher education was raised by just 21 percent, according to PBS. In addition, evidence shows that the school-to-prison pipeline primarily captures and affects Black students, which mirrors the over-representation of this group in America's prisons and jails.

How It Works

The two key forces that produced and now maintain the school-to-prison pipeline are the use of zero tolerance policies that mandate exclusionary punishments and the presence of SROs on campuses.

These policies and practices became common following a deadly spate of school shootings across the US in the 1990s. Lawmakers and educators believed they would help to ensure safety on school campuses.

Having a zero tolerance policy means that a school has zero tolerance for any kind of misbehavior or violation of school rules, no matter how minor, unintentional, or subjectively defined it may be. In a school with a zero tolerance policy, suspensions and expulsions are normal and common ways of dealing with student misbehavior.

Impact of Zero Tolerance Policies

Research shows that the implementation of zero tolerance policies has led to significant increases in suspensions and expulsions. Citing a study by Michie, education scholar Henry Giroux observed that, over a four-year period, suspensions increased by 51 percent and expulsions by nearly 32 times after zero tolerance policies were implemented in Chicago schools. They jumped from just 21 expulsions in the 1994–95 school year to 668 in 1997–98. Similarly, Giroux cites a report from the *Denver Rocky Mountain News* that found that expulsions increased by more than 300 percent in the city's public schools between 1993 and 1997.

Once suspended or expelled, data show that students are less likely to complete high school, more than twice as likely to be arrested while on forced leave from school, and more likely to be in contact with the juvenile justice system during the year that follows the leave. In fact, sociologist David Ramey found, in a nationally representative study, that experiencing school punishment before the age of 15 is associated with contact with the criminal justice system for boys. Other research shows that students who do not complete high school are more likely to be incarcerated.

How SROs Facilitate the Pipeline

In addition to adopting harsh zero tolerance policies, most schools across the country now have police present on campus on a daily basis and most states require educators to report student misbehavior to law enforcement. The presence of SROs on campus means that students have contact with law enforcement from a young age. Though their intended purpose is to protect students and ensure safety on school campuses, in many instances, the police handling of disciplinary issues escalates minor, non-violent infractions into violent, criminal incidents that have negative impacts on students.

By studying the distribution of federal funding for SROs and rates of school-related arrests, criminologist Emily G. Owens found that the presence of SROs on campus causes law enforcement agencies to learn of more crimes and increases the likelihood of arrest for those crimes among children under the age of 15.

Christopher A. Mallett, a legal scholar and expert on the school-to-prison pipeline, reviewed evidence of the pipeline's existence and concluded that "the increased use of zero tolerance policies and police...in the schools has exponentially increased arrests and referrals to the juvenile courts." Once they have made contact with the criminal justice system, data show that students are unlikely to graduate high school.

Overall, what over a decade of empirical research on this topic proves is that zero tolerance policies, punitive disciplinary measures like suspensions and expulsions, and the presence of SROs on campus have led to more and more students being pushed out of schools and into the juvenile and criminal justice systems. In short, these policies and practices created the school-to-prison pipeline and sustain it today.

But why exactly do these policies and practices make students more likely to commit crimes and end up in prison? Sociological theories and research help answer this question.

Institutions and Authority Figures Criminalize Students

One key sociological theory of deviance, known as labeling theory, contends that people come to identify and behave in ways that reflect how others label them. Applying this theory to the school-to-prison pipeline suggests that being labeled as a "bad" kid by school authorities and/or SROs, and being treated in a way that reflects that label (punitively), ultimately leads kids to internalize the label and behave in ways that make it real through action. In other words, it is a self-fulfilling prophecy.

Sociologist Victor Rios found just that in his studies of the effects of policing on the lives of Black and Latino boys in the San Francisco Bay Area. In his first book, *Punished: Policing the Lives of Black and Latino Boys*, Rios revealed through in-depth interviews and ethnographic observation how increased surveillance and attempts at controlling "at-risk" or deviant youth ultimately foster the very criminal behavior they are intended to prevent. In a social context in which social institutions label deviant youth as bad or criminal, and in doing so, strip them of dignity, fail to acknowledge their struggles, and do not treat them with respect, rebellion and criminality are acts of resistance. According to Rios, then, it is social institutions and their authorities that do the work of criminalizing youth.

Exclusion from School, Socialization into Crime

The sociological concept of socialization also helps shed light on why the school-to-prison pipeline exists. After family, school is the second most important and formative site of socialization for children and adolescents where they learn social norms for behavior and interaction and receive moral guidance from authority figures. Removing students from schools as a form of discipline takes them out of this formative environment and important process, and it removes them from the safety and structure that the school provides. Many students who express behavioral issues at school are acting out in response to stressful or dangerous conditions in their homes or neighborhoods, so removing them from school and returning them to a problematic or unsupervised home environment hurts rather than helps their development.

While removed from school during a suspension or expulsion, youth are more likely to spend time with others removed for similar reasons, and with those who are already engaged in criminal activity. Rather than being socialized by education-focused peers and educators, students who have been suspended or expelled will be socialized more by peers in similar situations. Because of these factors, the punishment of removal from school creates the conditions for the development of criminal behavior.

Harsh Punishment

Further, treating students as criminals when they have done nothing more than act out in minor, non-violent ways weakens the authority of educators, police, and other members of the juvenile and criminal justice sectors. The punishment does not fit the crime and so it suggests that those in positions of authority are not trustworthy, fair, and are even immoral. Seeking to do the opposite, authority figures who behave this way can actually teach students that they and their authority are not to be respected or trusted, which fosters conflict between them and students. This conflict then often leads to further exclusionary and damaging punishment experienced by students.

The Stigma of Exclusion

Finally, once excluded from school and labeled bad or criminal, students often find themselves stigmatized by their teachers, parents, friends, parents of friends, and other community members. They experience confusion, stress, depression, and anger as a result of being excluded from school and from being treated harshly and unfairly by those in charge. This makes it difficult to stay focused on school and hinders motivation to study and desire to return to school and to succeed academically.

Cumulatively, these social forces work to discourage academic studies, hinder academic achievement and even completion of high school, and push negatively labeled youth onto criminal paths and into the criminal justice system.

Black and American Indian Students Face Harsher Punishments and Higher Rates of Suspension and Expulsion

While Black people are just 13 percent of the total US population, they comprise the greatest percentage of people in prisons and jails—40 percent. Latinos are also over-represented in prisons and jails, but by far less. While they comprise 16 percent of the US population they represent 19 percent of those in prisons and jails. In contrast, white people make up just 39 percent of the incarcerated population, despite the fact that they are the majority race in the US, comprising 64 percent of the national population.

Data from across the US that illustrate punishment and school-related arrests show that the racial disparity in incarceration begins with the school-to-prison pipeline. Research shows that both schools with large Black populations and underfunded schools, many of which are majority-minority schools, are more likely to employ zero tolerance policies. Nationwide, Black and American Indian students face far greater rates of suspension and expulsion than do white students. In addition, data compiled by the National Center for Education Statistics show that while the percentage of white students suspended fell from 1999 to 2007, the percentage of Black and Hispanic students suspended rose.

A variety of studies and metrics show that Black and American Indian students are punished more frequently and more harshly for the same, mostly minor, offenses than are white students. Legal and educational scholar Daniel J. Losen points out that, though there is no evidence that these students misbehave more frequently or more severely than do white students, research from across the country shows that teachers and administrators punish them more—especially Black students. Losen cites one study that found that the disparity is greatest among non-serious offenses like cell phone use, violations of dress code, or subjectively defined offenses like being disruptive or displaying affection. Black first-time offenders in these categories are suspended at rates that are double or more than those for white first-time offenders.

According to the US Department of Education's Office for Civil Rights, about 5 percent of white students have been suspended during their schooling experience, compared with 16 percent of Black students. This means Black students are more than three times as likely to be suspended than their white peers. Though they comprise just 16 percent of the total enrollment of public school students, Black students comprise 32 percent of in-school suspensions and 33 percent of out-of-school suspensions. Troublingly, this disparity begins as early as preschool. Nearly half of all preschool students suspended are Black, though they represent just 18 percent of total preschool enrollment. American Indians also face inflated suspension rates. They represent 2 percent of out-of-school suspensions, which is 4 times greater than the percentage of total enrolled students that they comprise.

Black students are also far more likely to experience multiple suspensions. Though they are just 16 percent of the public school enrollment, they are a full 42 percent of those suspended multiple times. This means that their presence in the population of students with multiple suspensions is more than 2.6 times greater than their presence in the total population of students. Meanwhile, white students are under-represented among those with multiple suspensions, at just 31 percent. These disparate rates play out not only within schools but also across districts on the basis of race. Data shows that in the Midlands area of South Carolina, suspension figures in a mostly-Black school district are double what they are in a mostly-white one.

There is also evidence that shows that the overly harsh punishment of Black students is concentrated in the American south, where the legacy of slavery and Jim Crow exclusionary policies and violence against Black people manifest in everyday life. Of the 1.2 million Black students who were suspended nationwide during the 2011-2012 school year, more than half were located in 13 southern states. At the same time, half of all Black students expelled were from these states. In many of the school districts located in these states, Black students comprised 100 percent of students suspended or expelled in a given school year.

Among this population, students with disabilities are even more likely to experience exclusionary discipline. With the exception of Asian and Latino students, research shows that "more than one out of four boys of color with disabilities... and nearly one in five girls of color with disabilities receives an out-of-school suspension." Meanwhile, research shows that white students who express behavioral issues in school are more likely to be treated with medicine, which reduces their chances of ending up in jail or prison after acting out in school.

Black Students Face Higher Rates of School-Related Arrests and Removal from School System

Given that there is a connection between the experience of suspensions and engagement with the criminal justice system, and given that racial bias within education and among police is well-documented, it is no surprise that Black and Latino students comprise 70 percent of those who face referral to law enforcement or school-related arrests.

Once they are in contact with the criminal justice system, as the statistics on the school-to-prison pipeline cited above demonstrate, students are far less likely to complete high school. Those that do may do so in "alternative schools" for students labeled as "juvenile delinquents," many of which are unaccredited and offer lower quality education than they would receive in public schools. Others who are placed in juvenile detention centers or prison may receive no educational resources at all.

The racism embedded in the school-to-prison pipeline is a significant factor in producing the reality that Black and Latino students are far less likely than their white peers to complete high school and that Black, Latino, and American Indian people are much more likely than white people to end up in jail or prison.

What all of these data show us is that not only is the school-to-prison pipeline very real, but also, it is fueled by racial bias and produces racist outcomes that cause great harm to the lives, families, and communities of people of color across the United States.

| "*The private prison industry has long considered immigration detention an opportunity for gain.*"

Private Prison Contractors Profit from Immigration Enforcement

Livia Luan

In the following viewpoint Livia Luan argues that the private prison system has helped formulate immigration detention in the pursuit of profit. The largest corporations managing private prison contracts spend millions lobbying and contributing to political campaigns, with the hope that government policies will work in their favor and make them rich—or richer. Livia Luan is the programs associate and executive assistant at Asian Americans Advancing Justice (AAAJ).

As you read, consider the following questions:

1. What are some of the ways private prisons have helped form US immigration policy?
2. What laws and measures have increased the immigrant incarceration rate?
3. By what percentage did the company stock of private prison corporations rise as soon as Donald Trump was elected president?

"Profiting from Enforcement: The Role of Private Prisons in US Immigration Detention," by Livia Luan, Migration Policy Institute, May 2, 2018. Reprinted by permission.

The last few decades have witnessed the rising involvement and influence of the private prison industry in US immigration enforcement, alongside the expansion of the immigration detention system. During fiscal year (FY) 2016, approximately 353,000 immigrants identified for detention or removal by US Immigration and Customs Enforcement (ICE) passed through one of more than 200 immigration detention facilities, up from 209,000 in 2001. As of August 2016, nearly three-quarters of the average daily immigration detainee population was held in facilities operated by private prison companies—a sharp contrast from a decade ago, when the majority were held in ICE-contracted bedspace in local jails and state prisons.

The largest private prison contractors reap sizeable annual profits from detaining immigrants, including those identified for removal, asylum seekers and others awaiting a hearing in immigration court, and those in the process of being deported. CoreCivic, Inc. and GEO Group, Inc.—which collectively manage more than half of private prison contracts in the country (including immigration and nonimmigration detention)—earned combined revenue exceeding $4 billion in FY 2017. They have spent millions of dollars on lobbying and campaign contributions, seeking to sway the political process toward detention-focused policies that favor their interests—a tactic that appears to be paying off in the Trump era.

This article examines the economics of immigration detention in the United States, by focusing on the role of the private prison industry in immigration enforcement and policy. It explores the history and impact of immigration detention, the involvement of private prison companies, the effect of Obama administration immigration priorities on industry interests, and current and future opportunities for gain under the Trump administration.

History and Impact of Immigration Detention

Immigration detention is the practice of jailing noncitizens while they are in removal proceedings. The practice originated in 1882, with the creation of a federal immigration inspection system. Since immigration offenses violate civil rather than criminal law, deportation represents an administrative procedure enforcing the return of individuals who fail to comply with the conditions of their visas, according to the 1893 Supreme Court decision in *Fong Yue Ting vs. United States*. It is, therefore, different from the criminal justice system, which is correctional in nature.

Despite this important distinction, immigration detention grew harsher throughout the 20th century. Over the years, detention was used to ensure the thorough pre-entry inspection of European arrivals, to exclude Asian immigrants, and to imprison suspected anarchists, Bolsheviks, and labor organizers in the name of national security. Today, the standards governing detention facilities are based on those used for jails and pretrial prisons in the criminal justice system.

In the 1980s and beyond, increasingly broad detention practices culminated in the establishment of the mandatory detention statute—a series of policies requiring the incarceration of certain noncitizens without an individualized assessment. In 1988, motivated by the Reagan administration's escalation of the "war on drugs," Congress passed the Anti-Drug Abuse Act, which mandated the detention of any noncitizen convicted of an aggravated felony. Though this definition initially referred to serious crimes such as murder and drug trafficking, Congress soon expanded it to encompass other offenses, driving an increase in the average daily detainee population from less than 5,000 in 1985 to 7,500 in 1995.

Congress intensified its focus on mandatory detention following the 1993 World Trade Center bombing. The 1996 Antiterrorism and Effective Death Penalty Act (AEDPA) and Illegal Immigration Reform and Immigrant Responsibility Act of 1996 (IIRIRA) defined additional crimes as aggravated felonies for the purposes of immigration, including some nonviolent misdemeanors, and reduced the minimum potential prison sentence to be instantly deportable from five years to one year. In addition to removing many of the legal hurdles that had reprieved noncitizens from expedited deportation, AEDPA and IIRIRA curtailed judicial review and due process in immigration cases and restricted grants of relief for immigrants with family ties in the United States. Detention rates quickly rose as a result: The average daily detainee population nearly tripled compared to 1995, reaching 20,500 in FY 2001.

The 9/11 terrorist attacks cemented the securitization of immigration enforcement and policy. In 2002, the Homeland Security Act abolished the Immigration and Naturalization Service (INS), situating its functions within a new Department of Homeland Security (DHS) formed from the merger of 22 separate federal agencies. Three DHS components were created to oversee immigration: ICE, US Citizenship and Immigration Services (USCIS), and US Customs and Border Protection (CBP). In addition to broadening the use of nationality-based screening and enforcement programs, Congress further widened the category of people subject to mandatory detention. By doing so, it enabled criminal prosecution of immigration offenses and propelled the dramatic expansion of and investment in immigration detention.

Further, in 2004, Congress enacted the Intelligence Reform and Terrorism Prevention Act, which required DHS to expand detention capacity by 8,000 beds per year from FY 2006 through FY 2010, paving the way for greater numbers of people to be held. And in FY 2010, Congress tied DHS funding to satisfying the immigration bed quota, which was initially set at 33,400 beds per day; this rose to 34,000 in FY 2012, where it remained until quota language was omitted from the FY 2017 appropriations bill. Nearly 2.5 million immigrants have passed through immigration detention since 2003.

Emergence and Role of Private Prisons

It has become increasingly evident that the implementation of the mandatory detention statute has depended on the private prison industry. In response to the broader prison overcrowding that accompanied the rise of mass incarceration during the 1980s and 1990s, several states entered arrangements with private companies for their ability to build prisons quickly—and without the need for voter approval. Over time, privatization, combined with the political appeal of locking up large numbers of criminals, produced the "prison industrial complex"—a set of bureaucratic, political, and economic interests that encourage increased spending on imprisonment.

The private prison industry has long considered immigration detention an opportunity for gain. In 1984, CoreCivic established its first privately owned detention facility in Houston to hold immigration detainees. While the INS, and then DHS, at first had sufficient bed space in their own facilities to accommodate detainees, they later entered into several types of contracting arrangements to house the growing detainee population. These ranged from Intergovernmental Service Agreements (IGSAs) with state prisons and local jails, to contracts with alternative-detention facilities. DHS has relied heavily on IGSAs, through which 350 state prisons and local jails held 68 percent of detainees in January 2009.

In 2015, the private prison industry operated 62 percent of immigration detention beds and ran nine of the ten largest detention centers housing ICE detainees. Although the model of prison privatization varies, a private prison typically charges a daily rate per person incarcerated to cover investment and operating costs, and to turn a profit. In FY 2017, DHS spent approximately $126 per day for each detained noncitizen. As immigration detention costs steadily increased to around $2 billion annually, industry profits soared. Between 2007 and 2014, CoreCivic's overall annual profits grew from about $133 million to $195 million, and GEO Group's profits grew from about $42 million to $144 million yearly.

Proponents of private detention argue that competition improves quality while lowering costs; so far no substantial evidence has corroborated these claims. In fact, cost-saving measures often involve reduction of staffing, training, and programming, which results in poorer facility conditions. In 2016, in a move later rescinded by the Trump administration, the Justice Department announced the federal Bureau of Prisons (BOP) would not renew its contracts with private prison contractors, arguing that private facilities "compare poorly" to federal ones. The BOP identified serious or systemic safety and security deficiencies at private prisons, and these facilities have experienced more incidents per capita than BOP institutions. Further, the extent of competition is minimal: The three largest companies (CoreCivic, GEO Group, and Management and Training Corporation) account for more than 96 percent of the total number of private prison beds.

Over the past two decades, human-rights abuses within the immigration detention system have disproportionately occurred in private prisons. Among the 179 detainees in ICE custody who died between October 1, 2003 and February 19, 2018, 15 were housed in the CoreCivic-operated Eloy Federal Contract Facility in Arizona. A 2014 investigation of five of the nation's 13 Criminal Alien Requirement prisons, which are privately managed, found that the companies not only placed excessive numbers of prisoners in isolation, but also overcrowded the prisons, reduced medical staff, and withheld medical treatment. The same year, a lawsuit was filed on behalf of nine detainees at Aurora Detention Facility in Colorado against GEO Group, accusing the company of forcing detainees to work without pay and threatening them with solitary confinement if they refused. Further, a March 2018 report on abuses against African detainees at the West Texas Detention Facility, operated by LaSalle Corrections, documents excessive use of force as punishment, unsafe and unsanitary conditions, and denial of religious accommodation, among other concerns.

Obama Administration: Attempts at Reform, Followed by Expansion

A movement to reform the immigration detention system occurred early on during the Obama administration. In August 2009, ICE announced its decision to overhaul the system in order to create a "truly civil detention system." Beyond establishing the Office of Detention Policy and Planning, ICE created an online detainee locator system, reduced the number of contracts with private prisons, and deployed new field medical coordinators to all ICE field offices. New standards released in 2012 strengthened the process for filing complaints and stated that in deciding where to accommodate new detainees, ICE officers should give "special consideration" to factors that could make individuals vulnerable to abuse. Moreover, the agency deepened its investment in alternatives to detention (ATD), such as monitoring technology and home visits, increasing its funding request for this program from $72 million in FY 2012 to $111.6 million in FY 2013. Despite these changes, standards continued to be based on those used for individuals awaiting criminal trial, and ATD resources such as ankle bracelets represented a fraction of overall DHS custody operations funding; as a result, most detainees were still accommodated in jails or jail-like facilities.

Meanwhile, immigration enforcement reached a peak during the first few years of the Obama administration, with record numbers of arrests and removals. The Secure Communities information-sharing program in state prisons and local jails permitted fingerprint checks against DHS databases and interviews regarding immigration status, bringing ICE referrals for detention and removal to all-time highs. FY 2012 marked a peak of more than 464,000 immigrants cycling through detention facilities.

In its final years, the Obama administration narrowed its immigration enforcement focus, tightly prioritizing criminals, recent unauthorized border crossers, and those with recent removal orders. Following this refinement of priorities, arrests

THE COST OF CHILD DETENTION CAMPS

The Trump administration has been holding migrant children—whether they came to the US alone or were forcibly separated from their guardians—in a network of makeshift tent camps since last summer. An unnamed official at the Department of Health and Human Services told NBC News that housing costs $775 per child per day.

That's more than a $675 deluxe guest room at the Trump International Hotel in Washington, D.C.

Maintenance reportedly eats up most of the $775 daily cost per child for the tent camps, since it's difficult to keep temporary structures suitable for humans in a desert. In permanent facilities run by Health and Human Services, the cost is $256 per person per night, and NBC News estimates that even keeping children with their parents and guardians in Immigration and Customs Enforcement facilities would only cost $298 per night.

Even at the permanent facilities, there are questionable circumstances beyond costs, like a lack of soap and blankets. Clinical-law professor Warren Binford interviewed child detainees at a facility in Clint, Texas, telling Isaac Chotiner at *The New Yorker*, "They told us that they were hungry. They told us that some of them

and removals fell and immigration detention dropped to roughly 307,000 admissions in FY 2015.

This occurred against the backdrop of the decline of the federal criminal justice system's prison population, the result of new sentencing guidelines and reformed drug policies. The system contracted from 219,300 federal inmates at its peak in 2013 to 184,000 by the end of 2017, meaning reduced opportunities for private prison companies. Although the Justice Department's refusal to renew BOP contracts did not impact immigration detention, since ICE is housed within DHS, it further threatened the industry. On the day in August 2016 that the Justice Department announced it would not extend further contracts, GEO Group and CoreCivic stock values fell by 39 percent and more than 35 percent, respectively.

had not showered or had not showered until the day or two days before we arrived. Many of them described that they only brushed their teeth once...one of the reasons why we came back for a fourth day is that some of the children, on Wednesday, told us that there was a lice infestation, as well as an influenza outbreak ..."

Like the prison industry for the US criminal justice system, private companies can make a lot of money in the immigrant-detention business. Private-prison firm Geo Group has reportedly already made $500 million from migrant detention centers since Trump's "zero tolerance policy" began, as reported by the *Miami New Times*. Southwest Key Programs, a nonprofit that set up a boys' shelter in the husk of an old Walmart, reportedly netted $955 million in federal contracts between 2015 and 2018, according to *The New York Times*. A network of nonprofit groups, BCFS, reportedly received $179 million in the same time period.

As the *Texas Tribune* reports, since the filthy conditions at child detention centers went public, people in Texas have been collecting donations of diapers, soap, and toothbrushes. So far, Customs and Border Protection has refused to accept the donations.

"Trump's Child Detention Camps Cost $775 Per Person Every Day," by Luke Darby, Condé Nast, June 25, 2019.

Growing Political Involvement

Confronted with these challenges, private prison companies have significantly increased their political engagement. In order to influence immigration and criminal justice policy, the private prison industry primarily uses three strategies: contributing to political campaigns (via donations from individual employees or affiliated groups), lobbying, and building relationships, networks, and associations.

The growth of the first strategy is particularly noteworthy. Over the course of five election cycles between 2002 and 2010, state-level political giving by the three largest private prison firms increased from about $850,000 to more than $2 million. CoreCivic contributions by PACs and employees to federal candidates and outside groups increased from just $6,000 in the 1990 election cycle to roughly $249,000 in 2016, according to numbers from the Center for Responsive Politics. GEO Group has emerged as an even bigger contributor at the federal level, donating more than $1.2 million in the 2016 cycle, up from about $139,000 in 2004. The company has also spent growing amounts to lobby Congress—from $120,000 in 2004 to $1 million in 2016. CoreCivic spent $10.6 million on immigration-related lobbying between 2008 and 2014, according to a tally by Grassroots Leadership; of this total, $9,760,000 went toward directly lobbying members of the House Appropriations Committee Homeland Security Subcommittee, which is responsible for funding immigration detention.

The 2016 presidential election was critical to the private prison industry's interests. While Democratic presidential nominee Hillary Clinton expressed her intention to shut down federal contracts for all private prisons, Republican nominee Donald Trump praised the industry on the campaign trail. In addition, Clinton favored more lenient policies toward unauthorized immigrants, compared to the more hardline approach espoused by her opponent.

Private prison companies increased their political engagement during the election. One day after the Justice Department announcement about scaling back the use of private prisons, GEO Group donated $100,000 through a subsidiary to Rebuilding America Now, a pro-Trump super PAC. It gave another $125,000 to the same super PAC one week before the election. According to a spokesperson, CoreCivic did not contribute directly to any presidential candidates or campaigns during the election cycle, but it and GEO Group both donated $250,000 to the Trump inaugural committee.

Since the election, the industry has further accelerated its political activity. GEO Group spent $1.7 million on lobbying in 2017, a more than 70 percent increase from 2016, to promote issues including the deportation of federal prisoners and alternatives to detention within ICE. Both GEO Group and

CoreCivic have contributed to House and Senate candidates in the 2018 cycle.

And in addition to the donations to President Trump's inaugural committee, GEO Group moved its annual conference to the Trump National Doral Golf Club in Miami.

Business Booms under the Trump Administration

Placing their bet on the Trump administration appears to be paying off for private prison companies. A day after the election, GEO Group stock prices rose 21 percent and CoreCivic stocks soared by 43 percent. Shortly after his inauguration, President Trump signed two executive orders that benefit private prison interests. Executive Order 13767 included plans to tighten enforcement along the US-Mexico border, increase the use of detention in order to end "catch and release" of migrants pending their removal hearings, and expand detention capacity. The desired scale of this expansion was revealed in a leaked White House memo calling for a doubling of people in immigration detention to 80,000 per day. Further, Executive Order 13768 reversed Obama-era policies by prioritizing all unauthorized immigrants for enforcement, in addition to reviving Secure Communities and pushing for new agreements allowing state and local law enforcement to enter into partnerships to assist ICE in immigration enforcement.

The private prison industry predicts greater profits due to an increase in ICE arrests within the country's interior as compared to the level during the latter Obama years. Since removals in the US interior take longer to process, immigrants could spend longer periods of time in detention—a fact cited by CoreCivic and GEO Group officials as a source of optimism during separate earnings calls in August 2017.

In February 2017, Attorney General Jeff Sessions signaled renewed opportunities for private prison contractors by rescinding the Obama-era Justice Department memo intended to wind down the use of private prisons by BOP. By the end of the month, CoreCivic and GEO Group stocks had increased by 137 percent and 98 percent, respectively. In April, GEO Group won a $110 million contract to build the first detention center under the new administration, and ICE extended its contract with CoreCivic for a 1,000-bed immigrant processing center in Texas. In October, ICE issued a request for information about potential locations for up to 3,000 new detention beds within 180 miles of Chicago, Detroit, Salt Lake City, and St. Paul, Minnesota. Immigrant-rights advocates are bracing for widespread contracting activity beyond these developments, and efforts to push back on expanded detention have seen some success: California Governor Jerry Brown signed a bill in October 2017 blocking local authorities in the state from renewing or entering into contracts with for-profit companies to detain immigrants.

On February 27, 2018, the US Supreme Court ruled in *Jennings v. Rodriguez* that noncitizens, including asylum seekers and legal permanent residents identified for removal, do not have the right to periodic bond hearings. Although advocates contend that many of these noncitizens have a right to be released on bail until their case is heard, Justice Samuel A. Alito Jr., writing for the majority, argued that their detention was necessary to give officials time "to determine an alien's status without running the risk of the alien's either absconding or engaging in criminal activity." The decision reversed a Ninth US Circuit Court of Appeals ruling, but the case could return to the Supreme Court; for now, long-term detention will continue, at the same time as Trump administration policy assures detention will take place in more cases.

A Shared Goal

Private prison companies have already seen opportunities for expansion under the Trump administration and are projected to see more, so long as the administration pursues its goal of arresting, detaining, and deporting more immigrants. However, the ability of ICE to expand detention capacity remains limited by what Congress is willing to fund. Despite the administration's request for 9,000 additional detention beds in the FY 2019 budget, Congress appropriated enough money for about 1,200 more beds.

As the industry continues to prioritize political influence as part of its long-term growth strategy, it contributes to the growing privatization of the immigration detention system and solidifies the punitive nature of US immigration enforcement and policymaking. The administration's stiff enforcement policies and other moves signify rising profits and, at least for now, guarantee continuity.

Periodical and Internet Sources Bibliography

The following articles have been selected to supplement the diverse views presented in this chapter.

Daryl V. Atkinson, "A Revolution of Values in the US Criminal Justice System," Center for American Progress, February 27, 2018, https://www.americanprogress.org/issues/criminal -justice/news/2018/02/27/447225/revolution-values -u-s-criminal-justice-system/.

Paula Finn, "Nativism and the Immigration Industrial-Complex," New Labor Forum, May 2019, https://newlaborforum.cuny .edu/2019/05/29/nativism-and-the-immigration-industrial -complex/.

Madison Pauly, "Jail Inmates Worked for a $16 Billion Company Without Pay. Now They Want Their Wages," Mother Jones, January 6, 2020, https://www.motherjones.com/crime -justice/2020/01/alameda-santa-rita-jail-aramark-unpaid -wages-lawsuit/.

Val Reynoso, "Private Prisons in US Turn a Profit, Ruin Black Lives," telesur.net, October 25, 2017, https://www.telesurenglish.net /opinion/Private-Prisons-in-US-Turn-a-Profit-Ruin-Black -Lives-20171025-0011.html.

Robert Shirley, "What Is the 'Immigration Industrial Complex'?" Huffington Post, June 29, 2017, https://www.huffpost.com/entry /what-is-the-immigration-industrial-complex_b_5953b8cae4b0c 85b96c65e2c.

Morgan Simon, "SunTrust Joins Wave of Banks Exiting the Private Prison Industry," Forbes, July 8, 2019, https://www.forbes.com /sites/morgansimon/2019/07/08/suntrust-joins-wave-of-banks -exiting-the-private-prison-industry/#650c4703f630.

Christopher Zoukis, "From Cages to the Community: Prison Profiteers and the Treatment Industrial Complex," Prison Legal News, March 6, 2018, https://www.prisonlegalnews.org /news/2018/mar/6/cages-community-prison-profiteers-and -treatment-industrial-complex/.

OPPOSING
VIEWPOINTS®
SERIES

CHAPTER 4

What Is the Future of the Prison Industrial Complex?

Chapter Preface

T he prison industrial complex has deep roots running through all facets of the US economy. Activists and others that propose reform to the prison system plan to effect change by targeting the socioeconomic factors of those people most affected by the prison industrial complex.

They theorize that if they can change the issues that lead people to commit crimes, such as poverty, unemployment, homelessness, punishment rules and legislation, and immigration policy, among other things, then they can eliminate both crimes and the need for prisons.

The viewpoints in the following chapter explore the future of the prison industrial complex. Is the system so entrenched that there is no hope for change? Or is there a real opportunity for reform?

Viewpoint authors explore the prison abolition movement and the activist group the Formerly Incarcerated, Convicted People and Families Movement, who advocate for the full restoration of civil rights to those who have been imprisoned in the past. They rethink the harsh penalties, such as school suspension, that can lead to social disruption in lives of young people, particularly students of color. They brainstorm more humane and less punitive methods of corrections that focus on rehabilitation with the goal of creating a better society rather than a vicious cycle that harms communities.

What is the future of the prison industrial complex? Is it so entrenched in our system that it can't be changed? The viewpoints that follow attempt to address these questions and more.

"Criminal justice is often described by academics and journalists as a pendulum that swings wildly between harsh punishment focused on retribution, and more lenient treatment focused on redemption or reformation."

The First Step Act Reflects a New Criminal Justice Consensus

Michelle S. Phelps

In the following viewpoint Michelle S. Phelps discusses the passing of a recent crime bill, the First Step Act, that had broad bipartisan support towards a more moderate approach to criminal justice. The author traces past crime legislation and notes that, contrary to popular belief, Democrats and Republicans have been in agreement much of the time. She emphasizes that, historically, government's intentions toward the incarcerated often seesaw back and forth. Michelle S. Phelps is an assistant professor of sociology at the University of Minnesota.

"Congress's First Step Act Reflects a New Criminal Justice Consensus, but Will It Reduce Mass Incarceration?" by Michelle S. Phelps, The Conversation, January 30, 2019. https://theconversation.com/congresss-first-step-act-reflects-a-new-criminal-justice-consensus-but-will-it-reduce-mass-incarceration-109937. Licensed under CC BY-ND 4.0 International.

As you read, consider the following questions:

1. Is the author's tone hopeful about the First Step Act?
2. What is the pendulum metaphor used in this viewpoint?
3. Why do you think a more moderate approach to law enforcement has a broad bipartisan approval at this point?

When Donald Trump was elected president, many people feared his "law and order" campaign rhetoric would mean the end of criminal justice reform.

Trump confirmed this impression by appointing Jeff Sessions, an aggressive supporter of the "wars" on crime and drugs, to lead the Justice Department. Sessions quickly reversed a number of the progressive reforms introduced under President Barack Obama, including reducing penalties for drug offenses, ending private prison contracts, and investigating conduct of local police departments.

Yet by December 2018, Jeff Sessions had resigned and the federal government passed a criminal justice reform bill, the "First Step Act." The law reduces prison sentences, by changing the sentencing guidelines and facilitating early release, and supports education and treatment programs in prison.

The bill was supported by the White House, Republican and Democratic leaders, and an unlikely set of advocates from progressive non-profits like the Brennan Center and American Civil Liberties Union to the conservative Koch Brothers.

The following month, Trump seemingly reversed course again, appointing William Barr—another staunch supporter of the "tough on crime" approach—to replace Sessions.

How do we make sense of these seemingly contradictory developments and alliances?

I have found in my research that criminal justice policies and practices in the United States have often followed complex trajectories. Reforms often receive support from unlikely coalitions. But, by focusing on these strange bedfellows, commentators and advocates sometimes paper over the deeper disagreements in

PRIVATE FIRMS EARN BILLIONS FOR SERVICES TO THE INCARCERATED

A few businesses are involved in almost every aspect of prison life, taking in billions of dollars every year for products and services, often with little oversight, Axios reports. Taxpayers, incarcerated people and their families spend around $85 billion a year on public and private correction facilities, bail and prison services, says the Prison Policy Initiative.

For-profit prison companies started in response to the government's incapacity to handle the skyrocketing incarcerated population. They are "one more hurdle" to changing the system of mass incarceration, says Lauren-Brooke Eisen of the Brennan Center for Justice. About 80 percent of inmate phone calls go through Secarus or GTL, both owned by private firms and known for sometimes charging outrageous fees ($8.20 for the first minute, in one case).

The largest private provider of prison medical services is believed to be Corizon Health, operating in 220 facilities in 17 states and owned by a New York City hedge fund. Corizon was paid $15.16 per incarcerated person per day for medical staffing in Arizona's prisons, before being accused of cheating state monitors and losing the account to another private company.

Two companies—Aramark and Trinity Services—provide meals in around 800 state and local facilities. Michigan awarded a $145 million contract to Aramark, then fired the company for everything from "meal shortages to maggots in the kitchen," and replaced it with Trinity at an annual cost of $158 million. Problems persisted, causing Michigan to abandon privatized food services. Tennessee-based Prisoner Transportation Services is the largest provider of transportation for jails and prisons.

In 2016, it priced services to Nevada at $1.05 per mile, with higher rates for minors or those with mental disabilities. The minimum trip fee was $350. For-profit companies are expanding beyond prison walls, running re-entry programs, providing ankle bracelets and other monitoring devices for parole and probation, and operating immigrant detention.

"Profits & Prisons: Private Firms Earn Billions for Services to Incarcerated," The Crime Report, June 10, 2019.

ideas about who, how and how much to punish. Fights over these differences ultimately shape how policies get put into practice—and whether the bill ultimately achieves its intended outcomes.

While the First Step Act's passage may look like a clear victory for more moderate punishment, its implementation and impact under the Trump administration is likely to be quite limited.

Bipartisan Agreement on "Reform"

Criminal justice is often described by academics and journalists as a pendulum that swings wildly between harsh punishment focused on retribution, and more lenient treatment focused on redemption or reformation. In this metaphor, some people saw Trump's election as a swing of the pendulum away from progressive punishment and back toward punitive policies.

In our book *Breaking the Pendulum*, my colleagues Joshua Page and Philip Goodman and I argue that a better metaphor is the constant, low-level grinding of tectonic plates that continually produce friction and occasionally erupt in earthquakes. This friction manifests in traditional political combat, mass demonstrations, prison rebellions, and academic and policy work. Periodically, major changes in conditions like crime rates and the economy change to provide support and opportunities to one side or another.

These changes often bring together unlikely allies.

People typically associate the "law and order" approach to criminal justice with Republicans. However, new research shows how liberals laid the ground for these policies. It was the Democratic administration of President Lyndon Johnson during the 1960s that first launched the "war on crime" by expanding federal funding to build up the capacity of local law enforcement agencies. In the following decades, the crime rate spiked, due in part to better reporting by police departments, and crime became a hot political issue.

By the 1990s, Republicans and Democrats had all but converged on attitudes toward law enforcement. Not wanting to lose to Republicans by being portrayed as "soft on crime," Democrats took increasingly "tough" criminal justice stances. President Bill Clinton's wildly popular 1994 Violent Crime Control and Law Enforcement Act was the apex of this bipartisan enthusiasm for aggressive policing, prosecution and punishment. The bill made federal sentencing guidelines more severe, increasing both life sentences and the death penalty, and built up funding streams to increase local police forces and state prison capacity.

Despite the rhetoric of the crime bill, the best evidence suggests that it played little role in the explosion of the national prison population—or what scholars term "mass imprisonment." This is because policies focused on harsh punishment had already peaked by 1994. In addition, it only applied to the federal system, which represents only 10 percent of all people locked up. Finally, even though there was wide support for the crime bill, activists, politicians, judges and others continued to fight against "tough" punishment, eventually building the momentum for the First Step Act.

First Step Act

What does this history tell us about the First Step Act?

First, it's not surprising that Republicans and Democrats, conservatives and liberals came together on the bill. Both camps have moved away from the "tough on crime" mantra. Democrats now talk of "smart on crime" policies while some Republicans support the "right on crime" initiative. Both agree that aggressive policing and heavy criminal penalties for low-level offenses, particularly drug crimes, do more harm than good.

The rise of a new approach to criminal justice can be tied to a number of changes since the 1990s, including historically low crime rates, strained state and federal budgets and a growing awareness of the negative consequences of mass incarceration. Critically, a cadre of conservative leaders spent the past two decades working to change Republican orthodoxy on this issue. They frame mass incarceration as a fiscal and moral failure that wastes tax dollars and violates the Christian principles of "second chances" and redemption.

As a result criminal justice reforms have been spreading to red and blue states alike since the 2000s. After the 2016 election, advocates including Jared Kushner, and a slew of celebrities like Kim Kardashian West, have urged the President to embrace reform. These pressures ultimately succeeded in prompting the White House to support the First Step Act.

However, bipartisan consensus is not as seamless as it is sometimes portrayed. A group of Republican leaders remain aggressively opposed to these criminal justice reforms. And at the last hour, they nearly killed the First Step Act.

That takes us back to Barr—Trump's recent selection to replace Sessions at the Department of Justice. Barr was President George H.W. Bush's Attorney General. He is perhaps best known for endorsing a Justice Department memo arguing for "More Incarceration" in 1992. As recently as 2015, he vocally opposed federal sentencing reform.

During his confirmation hearing last week, Barr promised to "diligently implement" the First Step Act, but then backtracked to support Session's policies at the Justice Department, adding, "we must keep up the pressure on chronic, violent criminals."

Like the '94 bill before it, this indicates that the First Step Act will likely be more bark than bite. The First Step Act might provide relief to several thousand current federal prisoners. But Barr will likely follow Sessions and direct his prosecutors to seek the maximum criminal penalties against current defendants, including for drug offenses, limiting the impact of the First Step Act's sentencing reform. And the bill will have no practical effect on state prison systems, which in some cases have already embraced much more radical reforms.

While the First Step Act is a move in the direction of more humane and moderate criminal justice practices, I think it will likely b e a very small first step indeed.

| *"I hope to move our society past the sensationalism of crime and punishment to a realization of the damage this system inflicts on real people and our country overall."*

Formerly Incarcerated Leaders Are Paving the Road for Change

The Chan Zuckerberg Initiative

In the following viewpoint the Chan Zuckerberg Initiative offers an introduction to the organizations and individuals supporting the aims of the Formerly Incarcerated, Convicted People and Families Movement (FICPFM), a national advocacy platform working for the full restoration of civil and human rights for the formerly imprisoned. The Chan Zuckerberg Initiative's Criminal Justice Reform Program supports efforts to redesign the justice system with community health and safety at its core, and with those impacted— presently and formerly incarcerated people, crime survivors, families, communities, correctional officers, and prosecutors—at the center of its transformation.

"Formerly Incarcerated Leaders Are Paving the Road for Change," The Chan Zuckerberg Initiative, April 23, 2019. Reprinted by permission.

As you read, consider the following questions:

1. What are some of the organizations the Chan Zuckerberg Initiative has acknowledged and what specifically are these organizations' goals?
2. What did the passage of Amendment 2 in Louisiana accomplish? How may this impact the Prison Industrial Complex and/or formerly incarcerated individuals?
3. Do you think including formerly incarcerated individuals in advocacy leadership roles is necessary and important? Why or why not?

At the Chan Zuckerberg Initiative, we want to help the diverse and growing criminal justice reform movement flourish, which includes ensuring that those closest to the problem have the tools and resources needed to lead its transformation.

This year for Second Chances Month, we're proud to announce eight new grants to organizations not only led by formerly incarcerated individuals, but who are also working hard to ensure that people with histories of incarceration can actively participate in reform.

Voice of the Experienced

A grassroots organization founded and run by formerly incarcerated people, their families, and allies, dedicated to restoring the full human and civil rights of those most impacted by the criminal justice system. Norris Henderson is the Executive Director.

National Council for Incarcerated and Formerly Incarcerated Women and Girls

A group dedicated to ending mass incarceration of women and girls. The organization, led by Andrea James, runs a membership-based platform that provides technical support, complex coalition building, and comprehensive resources that assist local initiatives toward a shared goal.

Legal Services for Prisoners with Children

LSPC (All of Us or None) is led by Dorsey Nunn, and organizes communities impacted by the criminal justice system and advocates to release incarcerated people, to restore human and civil rights, and to reunify families and communities.

Forward Justice

A nonpartisan law, policy, and strategy center co-led by Daryl Atkinson, Forward Justice is dedicated to advancing racial, social, and economic justice in the US South. CZI is supporting their work to reduce incarceration and to advance Clean Slate reform specifically in North Carolina, which would automatically clear certain criminal records over time.

Florida Rights Restoration Coalition

The FRRC is a grassroots membership organization run by returning citizens—including their President, Desmond Meade—who are dedicated to ending the disenfranchisement of and discrimination against people with convictions.

Communities United for Restorative Youth Justice

CURYJ builds community relationships and mobilizes young leaders to organize and create the movement to end mass incarceration and youth criminalization. The group was founded by leaders who lived through the impacts of systemic violence and incarceration, and who set out to beautify their neighborhood, engage youth in the area and coordinate pro-bono legal defense for local defendants in the Fruitvale gang injunctions. George Galvis is the Executive Director.

College & Community Fellowship

Run by Vivian Nixon, College & Community Fellowship is an organization that enables women with criminal convictions to earn their college degrees so that they, their families, and their communities can thrive.

Anti-Recidivism Coalition

The mission of the Anti-Recidivism Coalition (ARC) is to change lives and create safe, healthy communities by providing a support and advocacy network for and by formerly incarcerated men and women. ARC, and Executive Director Shaka Senghor, advocates for fair policies in the juvenile and criminal justice systems and provides a supportive network and reentry services to formerly incarcerated individuals.

"I'm here now because I know that any movement has to be led by the people who are most intimately invested…they're the ones who've got skin in the game," said Daryl Atkinson, Co-Director of Forward Justice. "Together, we have to end the bad thing—mass incarceration and racial injustice—but we also have to set up an infrastructure where we can really have that beloved community that we want to see."

Many of these groups are also part of the Formerly Incarcerated, Convicted People and Families Movement (FICPFM), another partner of CZI. We celebrate the impactful work of FICPFM members, which includes the passage of Amendment 2 in Louisiana that did away with non-unanimous juries.

"I feel strongly that lifting up the collective stories of incarcerated people is my duty," said Aly Tamboura, Criminal Justice Reform Manager at the Chan Zuckerberg Initiative, who leads CZI's work with formerly incarcerated leaders. "I hope to move our society past the sensationalism of crime and punishment to a realization of the damage this system inflicts on real people and our country overall. I am sharing my own story honestly and openly, without shame or embarrassment, in the hope that it will inspire other formerly incarcerated people to recognize their own potential, and create fair chances for them to positively contribute to–and lead–our communities."

These new grants come on the heels of additional announcements earlier this month, celebrating CZI's support of organizations working to make real second chances possible.

"*Suspending a kid or sending them to the office is easy and quick. The things we're asking schools to do in place of those things are not easy and quick. The answers are complicated, and I understand teachers need resources and tools to make these changes.*"

It's Time to Shut Down the School-to-Prison Pipeline

Mary Ellen Flannery

In the following viewpoint, Mary Ellen Flannery argues that the recent tendencies of school districts to offer punitive measures rather than constructive solutions for students sends them down a path towards jail time. School suspensions not only interrupt learning; they can change the course of a student's life, influencing them to drop out of school, rely on social welfare, and even become incarcerated. The author highlights initiatives that help educators understand the repercussions of their actions and suggest alternatives to zero tolerance policies that fuel the school-to-prison pipeline. Mary Ellen Flannery is a senior writer and editor with the National Education Association (NEA), based in Washington, D.C.

"The School-to-Prison Pipeline: Time to Shut It Down," by Mary Ellen Flannery, National Education Association, January 5, 2015. Reprinted by permission.

As you read, consider the following questions:

1. How are excessive punitive measures setting up students for the school-to-prison pipeline?
2. How does the author say suspension hurts students beyond learning?
3. What is cultural deficit thinking?

Years ago, James Duran didn't think too much before suspending students who came to his office with stories of swearing at teachers, disrupting class, or even arriving late to school.

"I can tell you that I was suspending upwards of 300 kids a year. And I'll tell you, I'll admit it, that's just what we did in schools. We suspended kids," says Duran, the veteran dean of discipline at Skinner Middle School in Denver. "Looking back, it was a big cop-out. Basically it just gave kids permission not to be in school."

Duran wasn't the only one pushing kids out. In 2010, more than 3 million students were suspended from school, or double the level of suspensions in the 1970s. Meanwhile, more than a quarter-million were "referred" to police officers for misdemeanor tickets, very often for offenses that once would have elicited a stern talking-to.

The practice of pushing kids out of school and toward the juvenile and criminal justice systems has become known as the "school-to-prison pipeline," and in 2013, NEA members and leaders made a formal commitment to close it. Fueled by zero tolerance policies and the presence of police officers in schools, and made worse by school funding cuts that overburden counselors and high-stakes tests that stress teachers, these excessive practices have resulted in the suspensions, expulsions, and arrests of tens of millions of public school students, especially students of color and those with disabilities or who identify as LGBT.

For those students, it isn't just an interruption in learning, although it's definitely that, too—if they aren't in school, they aren't learning. A suspension can be life altering. It is the number-one predictor—more than poverty—of whether children will drop out of school, and walk down a road that includes greater likelihood of unemployment, reliance on social-welfare programs, and imprisonment.

"My eyes were opened by a young man I met who had spent 21 days in a juvenile detention center, basically for talking back in class," says NEA Executive Committee member Kevin Gilbert. "As educators, we need to step back and look at our discipline structures. We need to make sure they're going to help, not hurt students."

Consider the Maryland 7-year-old who was suspended in 2013 for chewing his Pop-Tart into the shape of a gun. Or the Michigan senior expelled in October for forgetting the pocketknife in her purse. Or the seven North Carolina teenagers who were arrested and charged with "disorderly conduct" in 2013 for an end-of-the-year water balloon fight.

Then there's Patricia Cardenas—a Denver high school junior. She didn't realize a warrant for her arrest had been issued when she was in middle school until she tried to get a driver's license last year.

"I had a really difficult time in middle school. My parents were getting divorced, and we were moving, and I was just a train wreck. One day this girl showed up from high school, and she came after me," says Cardenas. "When the cops came, this one teacher kept saying, 'Give her a ticket, give her a ticket!' I didn't think he had given me one, but I guess he did.

"Looking back, I know that teacher didn't like me, and honestly I think she was pushing me out," says Cardenas, who is active with Padres Unidos, a Denver community group that fights the school-to-prison pipeline. "Today my first priority is school and I've gotten it together. But it didn't used to be like that, and nobody asked me what was going on."

Let's Talk About Racism

According to the US Department of Justice, which last year ordered school districts to respond to student misbehavior in "fair, non-discriminatory, and effective" ways, Black students are suspended and expelled at a rate three times greater than White students, while Black and Latino students account for 70 percent of police referrals.

Also, students with disabilities are twice as likely to be suspended than their non-disabled peers, and LGBT students are 1.4 times more likely to face suspension than their straight peers. In Ohio, a Black child with an emotional disability was 17 times more likely to be suspended than a White, non-disabled peer. Combine these "risk factors," and you're talking about a child who might as well stay home.

The bias starts early. Black children represent 18 percent of pre-school students, but account for 48 percent of pre-school suspensions. Yes, we're talking about 4-year-olds.

"It's crystal clear that Black students, especially boys, get it worse," said Jacqui Greadington, chair of the NEA Black Caucus. "Studies have shown that a Black child, especially a male, is seen to be a bigger threat just because they are. They are. They exist."

In fact, according to research, Black students do not "act out" in class more frequently than their White peers. But Black students are more likely to be sent to the principal's office for subjective offenses, like "disrupting class," and they're more likely to be sent there by White teachers, according to Kirwan Institute research on implicit bias. (White students, on the other hand, are more likely to be suspended for objective offenses, like drug possession.)

The Kirwan Institute blames "cultural deficit thinking," which leads educators to "harbor negative assumptions about the ability, aspirations, and work ethic of these students—especially poor students of color—based on the assumption that they and their families do not value education." These racist perceptions create a stereotype that students of color are disrespectful and disruptive, which zero tolerance policies exploit.

LOUISIANA'S HIGH INCARCERATION RATE

Louisiana lawmakers will decide whether to enact changes proposed to shrink the number of people in prison and bolster programs aimed at keeping them from reoffending after they leave. Among the data and information included in the task force report:

Statistics:

- Louisiana has the highest per capita incarceration rate in the United States, with 816 people in prison for every 100,000 residents. That's nearly double the national average.
- Nearly 35,700 people are incarcerated today. The number of prisoners has grown 30 times faster than the state's population since the late 1970s.
- One in three people return to prison in Louisiana within three years of release.
- Louisiana sends people to prison for drug, property and other nonviolent crimes at twice the rate of South Carolina and three times the rate of Florida.
- Among those sentenced to prison in Louisiana, the top 10 crimes are nonviolent. Five of the top 10 are drug offenses. The most common is drug possession.

"I see it. I work in it. And I know it exists," says Betsy Johnson, a Montgomery County, Md., middle school teacher who co-facilitates an NEA GPS Network community group about school-to-prison pipeline issues.

"No one wants to put it on the table, but when we have those courageous conversations, when we deal with structural racism, and when we do look inward at our own biases and differences, we can begin to heal," says Johnson. "We can begin to understand. And when we begin to understand it, we can pass it down to our children."

For Georgene Fountain, a Montgomery County, Md., teacher who authored the 2014 revisions to NEA's formal policy on student discipline, which encourages the use of preventative discipline

- 81 percent of admissions to prison in Louisiana in 2015 were for nonviolent crimes.
- Louisiana's parole board heard 45 percent fewer cases in 2015 than it did 10 years earlier.
- Louisiana is spending $625 million this year for adult corrections, the state's third-largest spending area.

Task Force Estimates:

If the recommendations are enacted, the task force estimates in a decade:

- Louisiana's prison population would drop 13 percent from an expected 36,541 people to 31,724 people.
- The number of people on community supervision through probation and parole would drop 16 percent from an expected 69,250 people to 57,829.
- Caseloads for probation and parole workers would drop from an average of 139 cases per officer to 113 cases.
- Louisiana would save $305 million in corrections costs, though the task force recommends $154 million be reinvested into public safety and re-entry programs. Net savings would be $151 million.

"Louisiana Has the Highest Incarceration Rate in the Nation," Gray Digital Media, March 17, 2017.

and rehabilitative measures, the wake-up call came from Michelle Alexander, author of *The New Jim Crow: Mass Incarceration in the Age of Colorblindness.*

In her 2012 book, Alexander points out that nearly one in three Black men will spend time in US prisons. "When I [met Alexander] she looked me in the eyeballs and said, 'What is your organization doing about this?'" recalls Fountain.

The School-to-Prison Pipeline: What NEA Is Doing About It

In 2013, the NEA Representative Assembly, spurred by Fountain and others, committed NEA to end the school-to-prison pipeline.

Since then, NEA leaders and members have helped raise awareness of the issue, shape district and state policies, and provide resources on restorative practices.

"With education resources being cut nationwide, many educators are so caught up in trying to do more with less," says Gilbert, "and many are not aware that when they remove a student from the classroom, they may be unknowingly feeding the school-to-prison pipeline. We've got to make more educators aware and we've got to give them better tools and skills."

In 2014, the Montgomery County Education Association and superintendent worked together on a new student code of conduct that minimizes suspensions and allows students to learn from their mistakes. Meanwhile, other districts have signed "memorandums of understanding" with local law enforcement agencies that keep minor offenders out of criminal courts.

It's clear that suspensions don't really work. "They're a way to get the kid out the classroom, but that's a really short-sighted view because that kid is coming back," says Daniel Kim, an organizer with Denver's Padres Unidos, which helped win a 2013 Colorado law restricting use of suspensions and expulsions. (Since its passage, suspensions in Colorado have fallen by 25 percent, while school attendance and punctuality have improved by 30 percent.) Maryland also passed a similar law last year.

But it's also clear that educators can't just end suspensions and hope for the best. "We still have far too many situations where teachers are being assaulted, and it's not taken seriously," says Charlotte Hayer, president of the Richmond (Va.) Education Association. For teaching and learning to take place, schools must be safe and caring places, she adds.

To Hayer, the answers must include teacher training on cultural awareness and diversity. "You need to teach teachers how to build relationships with students who might not be like them," she says.

Recently, many teachers have been getting the training they need through increasingly popular "restorative practices," that help educators get to the root of disciplinary issues. Teachers using them often "circle up" with students when problems occur, which means having in-depth, facilitated conversations that force students to practice empathy and take responsibility for the way their actions affect others.

Last year, to help members master that process, NEA partnered with the Advancement Project, the Opportunity to Learn Campaign and the American Federation of Teachers to release a restorative practices toolkit. "Start by reflecting on your own practice, and what you do in your classroom," urges Harry Lawson, associate director of NEA's Human and Civil Rights department.

None of these answers are easy, acknowledges Sarah Biehl, of the Children's Defense Fund-Ohio, and the solutions are made more complicated by issues around high-stakes testing and funding cuts. In California, the average school counselor has more than 1,016 students on his or her plate. Meanwhile, the year-long standardized testing frenzy that occurs in US classrooms makes teachers anxious and stressed.

"Suspending a kid or sending them to the office is easy and quick. The things we're asking schools to do in place of those things are not easy and quick," Biehl says. "The answers are complicated, and I understand teachers need resources and tools to make these changes."

It's not easy or quick at Skinner Middle School anymore. This school year, James Duran has suspended just one kid. "Our approach is to keep the kids in, to do some kind of restorative approach, and maintain the attitude that 'you're going to school and you're going to learn,'" he says.

Just the other day, a student came to his office after cursing his teacher in the most offensive ways. "I really did it this time," the student announced. "You're going to have to suspend me, right?" he asked.

But Duran just chuckled. To the student's annoyance, Duran told him, "No, I am not suspending you. I'm keeping you here."

> *"The only way that society can ever progress away from the repressive actions of the penal system is to abolish it entirely and replace it with something else."*

Our Current Prison System Should Be Abolished

Red Sun in the Sky

In the following viewpoint Red Sun in the Sky argues that the prison system in the United States is so broken that it must be abolished altogether. The prison abolition movement acknowledges that the current prison system does not effectively address crime. Rather, it serves to keep a certain population down while others gain financially. The author suggests replacing the current system with one that concentrates on rehabilitation and restorative justice. Red Sun in the Sky is the personal blog of a writer who concentrates on history, politics, current events, and philosophy.

As you read, consider the following questions:

1. How does the author define prison abolition?
2. How does colonialism relate to the prison industrial complex?
3. Can punishment and rehabilitation go together?

According to a Pew Research Center report in 2008, 1 in every 100 Americans is in prison. In the United States, around 2,298,300 people are in the penal system out of a global prison population of around 9 million. Of the American prison population, 59% are either Black or Hispanic. Incarceration and punishment have long been thought to be the only solution to the issues of crime in both the United States and the world. This idea has led to the largest penal system in the world. The idea of prisons is so central to our society that it has become an accepted part of our collective psyche. Prison has become a figure equal to death and taxes in its inevitability and omnipresence. In many non-white communities in the United States, prison is a fact of life that continues to decimate families and the community. The very nature of many laws in the United States have intentions of incarcerating people of colour and keeping their communities down. Prisons have also become economically essential to the function of modern capitalism. From the private prison system to the prison industrial complex that provides cheap, almost slave labour to major corporations, the penal system has provided capitalism essential assets to continue its existence. Many people are aware of these outcomes but, many accept it as a natural conclusion or just a necessary evil. That is due to the normalization of prisons in our society, we are unable to conceive of an alternative. However, that is not the truth.

The solution is quite simple: Prison Abolition. The only way that society can ever progress away from the repressive actions of the penal system is to abolish it entirely and replace it with something else. This is because the system itself is far too large for simple reform to do much other than prolong its existence. Prison abolition not only strikes at the injustices of the penal system but, also those of capitalism and causes us to ask more questions about the way our society operates as a whole. These questions do not and never will have easy answers but, it is imperative that we ask them and try to find the answers. Especially when the questions deal with injustices within the very fundamentals of society for, when it comes to injustice, there is no room for complacency.

Before any discussion of prison abolition can begin, it must first be defined. Put simply, prison abolition is the abolition of prisons and while this definition is true, it lacks the essential context needed to understand it. There is a wealth of history, theory, and politics behind prison abolitionism. What prison abolitionism means is that the modern system of prisons in both the United States and the world at large does almost nothing at all to solve the systemic issues of crime. The system has from the very beginning only served the interests of the ruling classes in keeping certain subsections of the population interred, providing them with a plethora of cheap labour to exploit. Prison abolitionism also holds that the entire philosophy behind the concept of prison does nothing to actively solve issues of crime. The "prison as punishment" and deterrence policies of the US penal system has only fostered a backward and ineffective system that fails to solve the issues at hand while contributing to the racist structure of society. The growth of private interest in the prison system has also spurred discussion of prison abolition as a serious consideration. Private prisons in the United States make large profits from the states they reside in. Prisons also dominate societal and cultural landscapes. The popular conception of prison is one of something that always existed and will continue to exist. Prison abolition challenges that notion. Prison abolition challenges what society has accepted as a way to deal with its problems. It challenges economic structures, social relations, philosophies of justice, and the law. It is a critique of society as a whole.

The United States is a country founded on colonialism. The American War of Independence may have "freed" the country from the direct political control of colonial power but, the colonial structures continued to exist. Colonialism at its very core is a racist and repressive concept. It thrives on the repression of one group over another. Even after the war, the power structure continued to enforce itself. This is why some historians say that the American Revolution was not all that revolutionary. Those who started it were the white landed class and they maintained their power after, in fact even consolidated it. The ruling classes of the colonies wanted to retain their control of the economic assets that made the colonies successful. In much of the country at the time of the revolution, one of these major institutions was slavery. Another institution to arise around this time was that of the penal system. The new American nation needed to build up its laws and through them protect its institutions. This led to the intertwining of slavery and racism into the laws of the United States. Angela Davis in her book *Are Prisons Obsolete?* points out the many similarities between slavery and imprisonment. "…both institutions deployed similar forms of punishment, and prison regulations were, in fact, very similar to the slave codes—the laws that deprived enslaved human beings of virtually all rights." From this intertwining of slave and criminal policy came cultural ramifications as to which groups possess greater criminality than others. From the beginning of the United States, there has always been an association of black people with crime. This assumption has been solidified into law as a reflection of societal views. This started with the slave codes and those evolved into the so-called black codes following the abolition of slavery. The abolition of slavery through the 13th Amendment is a key landmark in the building of the prison system in the United States. The wording of the amendment is especially important. While it did abolish involuntary servitude and slavery, it had the exception of: "…except as a punishment for a crime whereof the party has been duly convicted." This laid the foundation for the current penal system and the establishment of penal labour camps. After the abolition of slavery, Southern states had begun to construct new ways in which to keep the white hegemony in the South. This was done through the previously mentioned Black Codes and later segregation. These laws provided broad definitions for crimes such as "vagrancy." These were intentionally vague so that they could be applied to black people. This grossly increased both the black prison population and the general view that black people were criminals. These trends and views are still present today in the societal standards we have today. A modern example of this would be the War on Drugs and how it failed to stop the drug problem but, did manage to disproportionally send non-white people to prison on petty drug charges. The War on Drugs was itself a racist endeavour. All one needs to look at is the 1994 interview with a former advisor to the Nixon administration, John Ehrlichman, where he said:

> The Nixon campaign in 1968, and the Nixon White House after that had two enemies: the antiwar left and black people…We knew we couldn't make it illegal to either be against the war or black, but by getting the public to associate the hippies with marijuana and the blacks with heroin, and then criminalizing both heavily, we could disrupt their communities…

Racial discrimination against black people is not the only form used by the penal system and prisons. Racism against Latinos, Indigenous groups, and Asians permeates the very core of the system. Angela Davis again states that "…racism surreptitiously defines social and economic structures in ways that are difficult to identify and thus are much more damaging." Racism, by involving itself in multiple facets of society becomes harder and harder to identify as the population is eased by a sense of normality. The prison system is ripe with this racism and it helps to get people into prison and repress them once they are inside. It should also be noted that the racism of the prison system is not limited to black people but, also all people of colour and immigrant populations. One notable example of this is the large amount of the prison population that is Hispanic and the mass arrests and harassment of people of Middle Eastern descent following 9/11 and the humanitarian travesty of the War on Terror. Racism is by no means the only issue within the prison system. Sexism and homophobia are also major forces within it. Women's prisons are notorious for a severe lack of resources and attention. Also, the system of punishment has tended to view female criminality as different from that of males. This led to an increasingly gendered prison system where the treatment of prisoners became unequal based on sex. In this case, women were often treated worse than men. Angela Davis points out a story from the Panther 21 trial in 1977 where Assata Shakur had been forced to stay in a men's prison while under constant surveillance. Another story from Shakur was when she was in a female prison in New Jersey. Here she says she was subject to an "internal search." This involved a nurse and a prison guard searching the vagina and other cavities of the prisoner. This was done with forced consent for, if the prisoner had refused the search, they would be sent to solitary confinement until they consented. Angela Davis, who had been in the same prison as Shakur, corroborates this story. This is but one of the many inhumane actions that can happen to female prisoners while in prison. Sexual abuse from prison guards is an all too common threat looming over the heads of female prisoners. A 1996 report from Human Rights Watch stated that: "…being a woman prisoner in US state prisons can be a terrifying experience." The patterns of abuse that exist within prisons are often tolerated by the system as the report also states: "Grievance or investigatory procedures, where they exist, are often ineffectual, and corrections employees continue to engage in abuse because they believe they will rarely be held accountable…" This pattern of sexual abuse of women also ties in with the rampant homophobia within the prison system. The patriarchal attitude of prison culture and the mindset of prison guards leaves LGBTQ+ prisoners vulnerable to abuse. Prison encourages the harmful male practice of machismo from guards which can lead to violence. All in all, many non-white and non-male prisoners feel the brunt of the injustices in the prison system, as it is built to repress those communities due to the latent ideology at play in the entire American justice and penal system.

Prisons are economic factors in society. As mentioned before, the 13th Amendment had abolished involuntary servitude in all cases except when it is punishment for a crime. The consequence of this is that corporations have been able to use the prison population as a pool of cheap labour in order to keep the cogs of capitalism moving. The classic image of the prisoners making license plates is how society has normalized the use of slave labour in the prison system but, this only scratches the surface. The entire system of prison labour is collectively called the Prison Industrial Complex (PIC). The PIC extends farther than just the use of inmate labour. It extends out into the construction of prisons, contractors that provide services to the prisons, and private prisons (which are possibly the worst idea anyone ever had). Private corporations rely heavily on the PIC in order for them to function properly. Jobs that were formerly given to union workers were switched over to prisoners. In the short essay "Masked Racism: Reflections on the Prison Industrial Complex," Angela Davis discusses why private business relies on prison labour. "For private business, prison labour is like a pot of gold. No strikes. No union organizing. No health benefits, unemployment insurance, or workers' compensation to pay." Major corporations use prison labour to do things such as data entry, call centres, and manufacturing. Within the Commonwealth of Virginia, much of the furniture used by the state government is made using prison labour. For all the work these prisoners put in, they get a pittance in return. In many states, prisoners are not even paid. This almost unlimited pool of slave labour has become one of the main cogs in the machine of modern capitalism. Davis again says: "Many corporations whose products we consume on a daily basis have learned that prison labour power can be as profitable as third world labour…" Davis continues to list some of the companies that use prison labour. Corporations such as IBM, Motorola, Microsoft, and Boeing are known to use prison labour. Clothing companies also use prison labour. The retailer Nordstrom had entire lines of clothes made in Oregon prisons. What the use of prison labour means is that companies begin to rely on it for a sizable portion of their workforce. This leads to a vested interest in keeping prison populations at a high level. This contradicts the supposed goal of the prison system and society itself of keeping the criminal population low. Direct labour is not the only way private interests profit from the PIC.

Private prisons are the natural consequence of the profit-motivated system of capitalism fusing with the corrections system. The private prison industry grew out of the government contracting services such as food and supplies out to contractors. This eventually evolved into private facilities. The primary issue with private prisons as a concept is that they are antithetical to the supposed goals of prison. A private prison company is in search of profit and needs to make one in order to continue to function. This means that in order for a private prison to exist, there must be a constant prison population. Private prisons are also notorious for the abuse of prisoners. The lack of oversight from state governments allows private prison guards and staff to get away with actions that government guards might not be able to get away with. The facilities themselves are also not kept up as well as other prisons. This leads to terrible conditions for prisoners interned there. One of the key problems with the private prison system is also the lack of facilities private prisons have. Medical treatment and mental health facilities are either underfunded or non-existent. This leads to cases of suicide becoming prevalent within the private prison system. Private prisons are the inevitable consequence of the role society has placed on prisons and the influence capitalism has on that system. As prisons become where society pushes its problematic members, the strain on the government grows. From there capitalism swoops in to try and fix all the problems but, ends up exacerbating them. Throw in also the fact that there are companies that do not want to see these problems fixed due to the pool of prison labour. These relationships form the basis of the prison industrial complex.

While the historical and economic reasons for prison abolition constitute enough to argue the point effectively, there is an entire another facet that is just as important: the philosophy. Prison functions on a philosophical basis of punishment and deterrence. This focus on punishment and deterrence overtakes rehabilitation, which should be the focus of correctional systems. What the punishment focus does is allow for recidivism and the inhumane practice of solitary confinement. The focus on deterrence allows for the usage of the death penalty and harsh punishment, such as the mandatory minimum laws that some states have. There also is the basic fact that: The denial of freedom does not foster free men. This notion comes from the belief that human beings have innate freedom and the want to be free. Denying said freedom is denying one of their humanity.

The focus of the prison system of locking up people and breaking their spirits in order to deter them from crime does very little to actually deter people. What it does is make them spiteful. The form of retributive justice that guides the prison system is not suited for a "rehabilitative" system. That is because punishment and rehabilitation cannot go together. It is either one or the other. This is because punishment does not help the criminal to reform themselves, it only gives them something to avoid. Take this as an example, say a child steals a cookie from the kitchen. The parents find out and punish the child by spanking him. After this, the child may refrain from stealing cookies for a while but, eventually may figure out ways to avoid the punishment. Another example is, imagine if, in lieu of spanking, the parents decided to ground the child and confine them to a room for a period of time. The child will become spiteful and will act out and steal again because it is constrained. Prison, as we know, has similar consequences. As the system develops new methods of punishment, criminals find new ways to avoid those punishments. If the criminal is caught, the harsh conditions of prison and the denial of freedom that goes with it will make them spiteful, more willing to strike out against the law once more. Mandatory minimums and harsh punishments do not stop crime, they make criminals more clever and less likely to reform.

Prison is a soul-crushing experience for a human being under any circumstance. That is the problem. People are crushed underneath authoritarian structures in prison and reminded constantly of what they did wrong but, never why they are wrong. Society sets out rules of which it governs itself by and those who break those rules must be told of that in some way. The problem every society confronts is as to how it should go about dealing with the criminal element. The most common way is through punishment, going all the way back to the Code of Hammurabi. It is from those early codes that we today form our conception of justice. This conception of justice as retributive is what makes many people opposed to true prison abolition and the introduction of rehabilitative methods. They feel that those who break the rules must always be punished to the most severe extent. It must be remembered that criminals are human beings as well. Rehabilitation works because it is philosophically sound with how corrections systems should work. It tells people why they are wrong and helps them to become better human beings and does not violate basic human rights. Rehabilitation seeks to reform the prisoner, not punish them. This being said, what of the victim? To many retributive justice works because the victims are satisfied that the criminal is getting their just consequences. That is where the concept of restorative justice fills the gap. Restorative justice is where the response to a crime is a dialogue. The prisoner is shown why what they did was wrong, the consequences that action had on other people and the community as a whole, and the criminal is then allowed to attempt reconciliation. That reconciliation is not an easy thing either. It could involve community service, compensation, or other methods. Another system of justice is that of popular justice. In popular justice, communities decide punishments for their criminals on a democratic basis. This concept is, however, not mutually exclusive with retributive or restorative justice but, is more of a method.

In essence, the main issue with the philosophy behind the mainstream conception of prison is that it lacks the humanity it needs. People upon entering prison are stripped of basic things that make them human. They are stripped of freedom, of rights, and basic needs. We have made solitary confinement, one of the worst things that can be done to a human being, a basic function of correction. The idea of corrections as having to be this stone cold and inhuman thing has led us to develop a form of totalitarianism within our prisons that makes it impossible for prisoners to even begin to reform themselves. We lock people up for years and then, without giving them a semblance of the proper resources to even begin to try and return to society, spit them out with full expectations that they will return. That is not humane.

Prisons also have very real material effects on people. Individual prisoners and the communities those prisoners come from all have to deal with the problems caused by the massive scale of the prison system and its byproducts. These issues have to do with the previously mentioned ideas of racism within the prison system and the disproportionate imprisonment of people of colour in the United States. The issue also has to do with the societal view of prison as something that can solve the problems of crime. Individuals that come out of prison are less likely to be able to reenter the workforce. This has tremendous effects on the person's family and community. The stigma society places on prisoners is what causes this. Due to the racist nature of the penal system, these adverse effects mainly affect communities of colour and poorer people.

According to the Southern Coalition for Social Justice, among black children in 2012, 1 in 9 have a parent in jail. Among Hispanic children, it is 1 in 28. The long-term effects of having a parent in prison are extremely harmful. Economically, it can lead to less money in the household which can lead to homelessness. Psychologically, it leaves children without strong parental figures. This leaves them in a place where they are susceptible to crime, drugs, and gangs. The economic instability will also drive them to crime and away from school. This is one of the many cycles that the entire system uses to perpetuate itself. Even after prisoners are let out and return to their homes and communities, the damage is already done. The mental and physical health of prisoners is one of the largest concerns after release. The APA states that approximately 10 to 20 per cent of inmates suffers from some sort of serious mental illness. On the matter of physical health, inmates often leave prison in worse shape than when they entered. This is due to the lack of proper facilities, quality of food, and generally poor quality of life in prison. When people are locked up, it takes away from their families a much needed economic assistance and when they return, they are not able to provide. The main obstacle many who are released face is the issue of societal stigma against prisoners. Employers will simply not hire released prisoners (but will exploit prison labour, funnily enough). What this leads to is recidivism. They will reenter prison. A report from the Congressional Research Service in 2015 put the percentage of prisoners who return to prison over a period of 5 years at 76.6 per cent.

These effects bleed over into the wider community as they are rocked by this happening to nearly every family. Communities find their young people gone, either in prison or somewhere else. Children become susceptible to criminal activity as their economic situation worsens and community leaders are left with very little power to stop it. This cycle keeps the systemic racism in place. It deprives people of colour the opportunity to function properly with the rest of society. This protects the interests of capitalists and government who know that if these communities that they exploit were to become conscious enough, would overthrow the existing system. This is also one of the main reasons why prison reform is almost a meaningless term when trying to look at real solutions to the problems caused by the penal system.

One of the main questions that will come up when one looks at prison abolition is something like: "These criticisms are great and all but, what is the alternative?" This question is a valid one but, also a very hard one to answer. Throughout the essay, there have been proposals of alternative methods such as alternative forms of justice or a focus on rehabilitation rather than punishment. These "alternatives" are rather unsatisfying for many as they are vague and that is intentional. Norwegian prison abolitionist Thomas Mathiesen wrote a book in 1974 called *The Politics of Abolition*. This book puts forward the key concept in prison abolitionism of "the unfinished alternative" or simply "the unfinished." What this means is that the alternative solution for the problems caused by prisons is not something that we can truly come up with before having abolished prisons. This is due to the weight the prison system has in society. We trust prison to deal with crime, mental illness, and it is tied to economic factors. No one person nor a small group of people could even begin to think of a working alternative. Mathiesen even states that is futile to try and think of a finished alternative. "...any attempt to change the existing order into something completely finished, a fully formed entity, is destined to fail..." Essentially, prison abolitionists cannot have a fully formed alternative in theory because it is not up to a small group to decide but, society as a whole. Rethinking prison means rethinking our culture, our economic system, and how we deal with our problematic elements of society. We have to rethink justice and all of our laws. It is not an easy road but, it is one that we must all take together.

Many will not be convinced by this essay. Many think that reform is the answer and that abolishing the prison system poses too many problems for society. Many will also object to the concept of the unfinished alternative. While the latter claim is a legitimate grievance that many can object to, it is hard to believe that such a system can be reformed. Reforming such a system that is so paramount to the functioning of societal repression is near impossible. The prison system as a functionary wing of capitalism helps to maintain itself. The only way to fix any of the major systemic issues described in this essay is to abolish prisons. Michel Foucault in *Discipline and Punish* put it best:

> One should recall that the movement for reforming the prisons, for controlling their functioning is not a recent phenomenon. It does not even seem to have originated in a recognition of failure. Prison "reform" is virtually contemporary with the prison itself: it constitutes, as it were, its programme.

> "The fact that private prisons have serious, documented flaws raises questions as to why the Trump administration is so eager to support them. It is noteworthy that a pro-Trump PAC and the president's inaugural committee have benefited from the private prison industry's financial contributions."

The Trump Administration Has Created Incentives for Increased Immigrant Detention

Hauwa Ahmed

In the following viewpoint Hauwa Ahmed argues that, while private prisons were on the brink of being phased out during the Obama administration, the Trump administration has breathed new life into them as immigrant detaining facilities. The author writes that these private prisons are dangerous for detainees, whose numbers have swelled due to Trump's immigration policies, but that they are incredibly profitable for many associated with the president. Hauwa Ahmed is a research assistant for Democracy and Government at the Center for American Progress.

"How Private Prisons Are Profiting Under the Trump Administration," by Hauwa Ahmed, Center for American Progress, August 30, 2019. Reprinted by permission.

As you read, consider the following questions:

1. What was the percentage increase of immigrants detained in for-profit facilities from 2000 to 2016?
2. How did Trump's election influence CoreCivic's stocks, according to the viewpoint?
3. Why are LGBTQ+ immigrants more vulnerable in ICE detention centers, according to the viewpoint?

There are more people behind bars in the United States than there are living in major American cities such as Phoenix or Philadelphia. According to a 2018 report from the US Bureau of Justice Statistics, nearly 2 million adults were being held in America's prisons and jails. Of these 2 million prisoners, about 128,063 were detained in federal or state facilities operated by private prison facilities, a 47 percent increase from the 87,369 prisoners in 2000.

In 2016, the US Department of Justice's (DOJ) inspector general initiated a review to examine conditions at a number of for-profit prisons that the federal government contracted with from fiscal year 2011 through fiscal year 2014. A report on the findings indicated that private prisons had a 28 percent higher rate of inmate-on-inmate assaults and more than twice as many inmate-on-staff assaults compared with federally run or operated prisons. Furthermore, the report found that for-profit prisons in the United States were more likely to endanger inmates' security and rights. These problems were so significant that in August 2016, the Obama administration announced that it would begin to phase out private prisons.

As the number of incarcerated individuals in for-profit prisons grew, so did the number of immigrants detained in such facilities. According to a report by the Sentencing Project, about 4,841 immigrants were detained in for-profit facilities in 2000. By

2016, that number had soared to 26,249 immigrants—a 442 percent increase. In the wake of the DOJ's decision to phase out the use of for-profit prisons, the Homeland Security Advisory Council reviewed the US Department of Homeland Security's (DHS) use of private immigration detention facilities. Immediately after this review was announced, the stock prices of private prison company giants CoreCivic—formerly the Corrections Corporation of America—and the GEO Group Inc. dropped by 9.4 percent and 6 percent, respectively. A majority of the council agreed with the view that DHS should begin to move away from using private prison facilities but recommended that while they were still in use, they "should come with improved and expanded [US Immigration and Customs Enforcement] oversight."

Following the inauguration of President Donald Trump in January 2017, however, the administration immediately shifted course to robustly support private prisons. In February of that year, then-Attorney General Jeff Sessions revoked the Obama administration's initiative, and by April 2017, the DOJ began requesting bids for contracts to house federal inmates in private prison facilities once again. That same month, the GEO Group won a $110 million contract to build the first detention center under the new administration.

The fact that private prisons have serious, documented flaws raises questions as to why the Trump administration is so eager to support them. It is noteworthy that a pro-Trump PAC and the president's inaugural committee have benefited from the private prison industry's financial contributions. The Trump family business has benefited from the industry's patronage as well.

This issue brief details how Trump administration policies have increased the migrant detainee population—and the profits of private prisons—as well as endangered the lives of migrants being held in detention. The brief then illustrates just how much money private prisons have spent in US political campaigns.

Trump Administration Policies Have Increased the Number of Migrants in Detention

The Trump administration has implemented policies that have increased the number of migrants in detention. In early 2017, President Trump signed an executive order titled "Enhancing Public Safety in the Interior of the United States," which instituted a massive expansion of immigration enforcement within the United States. It defined enforcement priorities so broadly that all undocumented individuals became subject to deportation orders, regardless of how long they had been in the country. The order represented a radical departure from the Obama administration's approach, which prioritized the removal of migrants who had been found guilty of crimes. The executive order also directed state and local police to enforce federal immigration laws.

Similarly, in April 2019, current Attorney General William Barr rescinded a decision that enabled eligible asylum-seekers to request bond from immigration judges. This decision effectively instituted indefinite detention due to the fact that some migrants will now be held in detention for months or years before their cases are adjudicated. Moreover, in July 2019, DHS increased its application of expedited removal, a fast-track summary process for deporting noncitizens without a hearing from an immigration judge.

Last week, the Trump administration issued a final rule in a legally questionable attempt to make changes to the 1997 *Flores* agreement, a long-standing legal agreement specifying basic standards of care for minors in detention. As interpreted, this agreement requires that minors not be held in unlicensed secure detention facilities for more than 20 days. If implemented, the administration's changes would effectively cause undocumented children and their families to be detained in inadequate, unlicensed facilities indefinitely. According to the president of the American Academy of Pediatrics, "no child should be placed in detention …

even short periods of detention can cause psychological trauma and long-term mental health risks."

As expected, the Trump administration's hard-line immigration policies have led to a record-high number of immigrant detainees. Currently, there are about 54,344 immigrants detained in about 200 detention centers across the country. In 2017, the last time ICE produced such data, more than three-fourths of the average daily detainee population was being held in a for-profit detention facility. CoreCivic and the GEO Group are recipients of more than one-half of private prison industry contracts. These companies manage the detention of immigrants seeking asylum, those awaiting hearings in immigration courts, and those who have been identified for removal. For every 100 immigrant detainees, 32 are in GEO Group facilities, and 21 are in CoreCivic facilities.

A record number of immigrants have died in detention. Since 2017, 27 immigrants have died in ICE custody, including a transgender woman named Roxsana Hernandez. Johana Medina Leon, also a transgender woman, died shortly after being released from custody. Of these 27 immigrants, 21 have died in facilities that are owned or operated by for-profit prison companies. In June 2019, the government's own investigators determined that conditions in major private prison facilities were "unsafe and unhealthy" and violated ICE's own standards. Despite these failures, the industry is benefiting enormously. Trump administration policies around enforcement priorities and detention practices have led to an increase in the demand for detention space, which has resulted in record-high profits for private detention facilities.

Under the Trump administration, ICE has significantly increased its enforcement operations, which has directly contributed to the rise in the migrant detainee population. In order to achieve this, ICE has consistently exceeded its budget. According to reporting from Buzzfeed News, there were 52,398 people in ICE custody in May 2019. Congress provided funds for ICE to maintain an average of 45,000 people in detention per day in the latest budget, but with about 54,344 migrants in detention currently, the agency is overspending these funds by more than 15 percent. DHS has also increasingly begun diverting funds that had been earmarked for other agency operations to ICE in order to fund enforcement and detention operations. According to a Roll Call report, DHS intends to divert more than $200 million from other programs—including disaster relief programs—to fund immigration detention. This is the fourth consecutive fiscal year in which DHS has repurposed funds meant for other agency operations toward immigration enforcement.

Significantly Increasing the Number of Immigrants in Detention Means Record-High Profits for Private Prisons

During his 2016 campaign, then-candidate Trump expressed support for expanding the role of private prisons and espoused hard-line immigration policies. The morning after his election, stocks in CoreCivic increased by 34 percent, and those in the GEO Group rose by 18 percent. The two companies have informed their shareholders that federal government contracts are integral to their profitability. In memos to their shareholders, both companies acknowledge that policies with the potential to reduce the US detainee population constitute potential risk factors to their business model.

Figure 1 indicates the extent to which both CoreCivic and the GEO Group are dependent on three government agencies—ICE, the Federal Bureau of Prisons, and the US Marshals Service—for their business.

In light of the fact that both CoreCivic and the GEO Group have depended on just three agencies charged with enforcement and detention operations for an average of about 48 percent of their revenues over the past two years, these two companies have a vested interest in the Trump administration's punitive immigration policies to ensure that they remain profitable.

Figure 1. Government Contracts Are a Major Source of Revenue for Private Prisons

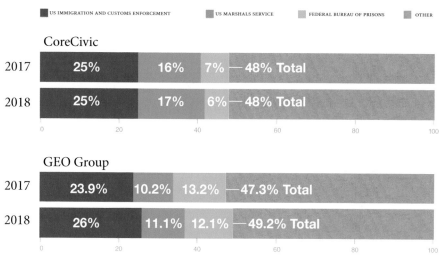

Source: US Securities and Exchange Commission

Conditions in Private Detention Facilities Endanger Immigrants' Lives

In FY 2018, DHS received $3 billion for custody operations. At least 75 percent of the detention facilities for which DHS contracts are privately owned or operated. Despite this level of funding, conditions at these detention centers remain dangerous, and detainees' rights are routinely violated. A 2019 Office of Inspector General (OIG) report on an investigation of ICE oversight of its contracted detention facilities indicates that the agency routinely waives its own standards, including those meant to ensure the health and safety of detainees. Additionally, ICE often fails to include its quality assurance surveillance plan (QASP)—a key tool for ensuring that facilities meet ICE's performance standards—in facility contracts and rarely imposes financial consequences for facilities that are noncompliant.

According to the OIG report, only 28 out of the 106 contracts reviewed contained a QASP. The report also stated that between October 1, 2015, and June 30, 2018, ICE imposed financial penalties on only two occasions despite documenting thousands of instances in which facilities failed to comply with detention standards. The OIG also investigated three GEO Group facilities and found "egregious violations of detention standards." All three facilities were found to have expired food, putting detainees' health at risk. The GEO Group-operated Aurora, Colorado, facility failed to provide recreation and outdoor activities to detainees. At another GEO Group-operated facility in Adelanto, California, the OIG identified detainee bathrooms that "were in poor condition, including mold and peeling paint on the walls, floors, and showers, and unusable toilets." All of these infractions violate ICE's standards.

According to a 2018 letter from the Office of Rep. Kathleen Rice (D-NY) to DHS, "Of the 298 transgender people ICE detained in FY 2017, 13% were placed in solitary confinement." This not only has adverse effects on detainees' mental health and well-being but is also against ICE's rules. While there is existing Obama-era guidance on how to provide care for transgender migrants in ICE custody, the guidance is not mandatory. Due to ICE's negligence, LGBTQ+ immigrants continue to face a higher risk of sexual violence than the general population. And as for-profit prisons continue to play an outsize role in immigration detention while providing substandard care, the health and safety of vulnerable populations such as LGBTQ+ migrants remain especially at risk.

Private Prison Companies Are Major Players in Political Spending

Although private prisons have been ineffective at providing high-quality detention services, they have been effective at supporting political allies. In the 2016 presidential election, for example, the GEO Group and CoreCivic donated $250,000 each to President

Trump's inaugural committee. In 2017, the GEO Group moved its annual conference to a Trump-owned resort in Boca Raton, Florida. Additionally, the GEO Group contributed heavily to the campaigns of some members of the US House Appropriations Subcommittee on Homeland Security, the congressional subcommittee charged with funding DHS.

These companies and their employees also contribute to congressional candidates, donating overwhelmingly to those running as Republicans. According to the Center for Responsive Politics, CoreCivic and its employees have spent about $3 million on campaign contributions to federal candidates and PACs since 1990. Eighty-five percent of CoreCivic's contributions to federal candidates since 1990 have gone to Republicans, while 13 percent of its contributions have gone to Democrats. Additionally, CoreCivic has spent $26.1 million on lobbying since 1998. The GEO Group and its employees have donated about $4.4 million to federal candidates and PACs since 2004. Since that year, 54 percent of the GEO Group's campaign contributions went to Republican candidates, while 15 percent went to Democratic candidates.

Conclusion

The Trump administration's immigration policies as well as existing immigration legislation create structural incentives to increase detention, which has largely been achieved through the use of private prisons. This increased role drives these companies' profitability while endangering the lives of immigrants through inadequate care and a lack of accountability. Special interests should not profit from immigration enforcement. Congress and the administration should hold private detention facilities that violate ICE'S standards accountable.

Periodical and Internet Sources Bibliography

The following articles have been selected to supplement the diverse views presented in this chapter.

Nora Ellman, "Immigration Detention Is Dangerous for Women's Health and Rights," Center for American Progress, October 21, 2019, https://www.americanprogress.org/issues/women /reports/2019/10/21/475997/immigration-detention-dangerous -womens-health-rights/.

Madeleine Joung, "What Is Happening at Migrant Detention Centers? Here's What to Know," *Time*, July 12, 2019, https://time .com/5623148/migrant-detention-centers-conditions/.

Emily Kassie, "Detained: How the US Built the World's Largest Immigrant Detention System," *Guardian*, September 24, 2019, https://www.theguardian.com/us-news/2019/sep/24/detained-us -largest-immigrant-detention-trump.

Sarah Kuta, "Stopping the School-to-Prison Pipeline Starts with Ending Suspensions," School Leaders Now, August 13, 2018, https://schoolleadersnow.weareteachers.com/end-school -suspensions/.

Los Angeles Times, "San Diego Librarian Collects More Than 1,700 Letters Written by Migrants in Detention Centers," December 16, 2019, https://ktla.com/2019/12/16/san-diego-librarian-collects -more-than-1700-letters-written-by-migrants-in-detention -centers/.

Andrew Moss, "Immigration and the Prison Industrial Complex," Counterpunch, January 8, 2020, https://www.counterpunch .org/2020/01/08/immigration-and-the-prison-industrial -complex/.

Brian Sonenstein, "It's All by Force': Formerly Incarcerated People Speak Out on Prison Reform," September 16, 2016, Shadowproof, https://shadowproof.com/2016/09/15/force-formerly -incarcerated-people-speak-prison-reform/.

Kodie Stoebig and Maria Marcelina Crystal Vega, "5 Ways to End the School to Prison Pipeline," SplinterNews.com, May 26, 2016, https://splinternews.com/5-ways-to-end-the-school-to-prison -pipeline-1793857087.

For Further Discussion

Chapter One

1. How is the prison industrial complex a reflection of classism and racism in America, and how is it related to the legacy of slavery?
2. What are further ways you can think of that the prison industrial complex is entrenched economically in society?
3. What are the pros and cons of prison work programs? Do you think they are effective policy in criminal justice?

Chapter Two

1. Do you think the War on Drugs is a disastrous policy? Why or why not? What alternatives can you see in policy for the future?
2. Do you think it is immoral to make a profit from the incarceration of human beings? Why or why not? Should morality be a consideration when debating the prison system?
3. How has legislation affected the prison system throughout US history?

Chapter Three

1. What large industries and banks have recently divested from the prison industrial complex? Do you see this a good move for society in the future? Why or why not?
2. How does the school-to-prison pipeline feed into the prison industrial complex? Have you seen examples of this in your school or community? How can this be damaging for a society?
3. How has current ICE policy and legislation affected the prison industrial complex and popular opinion about it?

Chapter Four

1. Do you feel the creation of the prison industrial complex is partisan or bipartisan as far as politics goes? Explain your answer using information from this volume's viewpoints.
2. What is the Formerly Incarcerated, Convicted People and Families Movement, and what is their message?
3. How do you view retributive justice vs. rehabilitative justice? What are some policy ideas you see going forward in changing the criminal justice system for the future?

Organizations to Contact

The editors have compiled the following list of organizations concerned with the issues debated in this book. The descriptions are derived from materials provided by the organizations. All have publications or information available for interested readers. The list was compiled on the date of publication of the present volume; the information provided here may change. Be aware that many organizations take several weeks or longer to respond to inquiries, so allow as much time as possible.

The Campaign for the Fair Sentencing of Youth

1319 F Street NW
Suite 303
Washington, DC 20004
(202) 289-4677
email: www.fairsentencingofyouth.org/contact-2/
website: https://www.fairsentencingofyouth.org/

The Campaign for the Fair Sentencing of Youth promotes advocacy, coalition-building, and public education to ban life without parole sentencing for youth and other extreme sentences for children.

The Center on Juvenile and Criminal Justice

424 Guerrero Street, Suite A
San Francisco, CA 94110
(415) 621-5661
website: www.cjcj.org

The Center on Juvenile and Criminal Justice (CJCJ) is a nonprofit nonpartisan organization working to reduce society's reliance on incarceration as a solution to social problems. It provides direct services, technical assistance, and policy designed to reduce incarceration and enhance long-term public safety.

Color of Change

email: www.colorofchange.org/contact-us
website: www.colorofchange.org

With 1.5 million members, Color of Change is the nation's largest online racial justice organization, helping people to respond to injustice effectively.

Critical Resistance

1904 Franklin Street, Suite 504
Oakland, CA 94612
(510) 444-0484
email: crnational@criticalresistance.org
website: www.criticalresistance.org

Formed in 1997, Critical Resistance is a national platform dedicated to building a movement to eliminate the prison industrial complex.

Ella Baker Center for Human Rights

1419 34th Ave, Suite 202
Oakland, CA 94601
(510) 428-3939
website: www.ellabakercenter.org

Named after Ella Baker, a hero of the civil rights movement, the Ella Baker Center works to shift resources away from prisons and punishment and toward opportunities that make communities safe, healthy, and strong.

Equal Justice Under Law

400 7th Street NW, Suite 602
Washington, DC 20004
(202) 670-1004
email: admin@equaljusticeunderlaw.org
website: www.equaljusticeunderlaw.org

Equal Justice Under Law is a nonprofit law organization dedicated to achieving equality in the criminal system and ending cycles of poverty across the nation.

The Innocence Project

40 Worth Street, Suite 701
New York, NY 10013
(212) 364-5340
email: info@innocenceproject.org
website: www.innocenceproject.org

The Innocence Project was founded in 1992 by Peter Neufeld and Barry Scheck at Cardozo School of Law. It works to exonerate the wrongly convicted through DNA testing and to initiate reforms in the criminal justice system to prevent future injustice.

The Last Mile

717 Market Street
Suite 100
San Francisco, CA 94103
email: info@thelastmile.org
website: https://thelastmile.org

The Last Mile is a nonprofit organization that works providing coding and technology training to the incarcerated population across the United States. It was founded in 2010 at San Quentin State Prison, California.

The Marshall Project

156 West 56th Street, Suite 701
New York, NY 10019
(212) 803-5200
email: info@themarshallproject.org
website: www.themarshallproject.org

The Marshall Project is a not for profit, nonpartisan news organization that hopes to bring a sense of urgency regarding problems within the US criminal justice system through award-winning journalism and other news and community platforms.

National Council for Incarcerated and Formerly Incarcerated Women and Girls

100R Warren Street
Roxbury, MA 02119
email: www.nationalcouncil.us/contact/
website: www.nationalcouncil.us

The National Council for Incarcerated and Formerly Incarcerated Women and Girls is dedicated to ending the incarceration of women and girls through a platform of technical support, complex coalition building, and resources shifting the criminal justice system to one based on human justice.

National Employment Law Project (NELP)

90 Broad Street, Suite 1100
New York, NY 1004
(212) 285-3025
email: nelp@nelp.org
website: www.nelp.org/campaign/ensuring-fair-chance-to-work/

The National Employment Law Project (NELP) seeks to ensure that America upholds, for all workers, the promise of opportunity and economic security through work by expansion of access to work, the strengthening of protections, and support for low-wage workers and the unemployed, including the formerly incarcerated.

Prisoners Literature Project

Grassroots House
2022 Blake Street
Berkeley, CA 94704
(510) 437 0257
email: Prisonlit@gmail.com
website: www.prisonlit.org

The Prisoners Literature Project is an all-volunteer, nonprofit group that sends free books directly to prisoners who request them from throughout the United States and has been in operation for nearly 30 years.

Project NIA

c/o CFS
719 S State Street
4th Floor
Chicago, IL 60605
(234) 567-8901
email: info@project-nia.com
website: www.project-nia.org

Project NIA is a grassroots organization based in Chicago that works to end the arrest and detention of children and young adults by promoting restorative and transformative justice practices.

The Sentencing Project

1705 DeSales Street NW
8th Floor
Washington, DC 20036
(202) 628-0871
email: staff@sentencingproject.org
website: www.sentencingproject.org

The Sentencing Project works for a fair and effective US criminal justice system through reforms in sentencing policy addressing unjust racial disparities and practices, and by advocating for alternatives to incarceration. It was founded in 1986.

Zehr Institute for Restorative Justice

Eastern Mennonite University
1200 Park Road
Harrison, VA 22802
(540) 432-4490
email: info@zehr-institute.org
website: https://zehr-institute.org

The Zehr Institute for Restorative Justice is a program of the Center for Justice and Peacebuilding at Eastern Mennonite University, advocating restorative justice as a social movement. It was founded in 2012.

Bibliography of Books

Alexander, Michelle. *The New Jim Crow: Mass Incarceration in the Age of Colorblindness.* New York: The New Press, 2012.

Bailey, Isaac J. *My Brother Moochie: Regaining Dignity in the Face of Crime, Poverty, and Racism in the American South.* New York: Other Press, 2018.

Bazelon, Emily. *Charged: The New Movement to Transform American Prosecution and End Mass Incarceration.* New York: Random House, 2019.

Berger, Dan, and Toussaint Losier (contributor). *Rethinking the American Prison Movement.* Abingdon-on-Thames, England: Routledge, 2017.

Bovan, Richard. *The Dedicated Ex-Prisoner's Guide to Life and Success on the Outside: 10 Rules for Making It in Society After Doing Time.* Memphis, TN: Full Surface Publishing, 2018.

CR10 Publications Collective, editors. *Abolition Now!: Ten Years of Strategy and Struggle Against the Prison Industrial Complex.* Chico, CA: AK Press, 2008.

Davis, Angela. *Are Prisons Obsolete?* New York: Seven Stories Press, 2003.

Davis, Angela. *The Prison Industrial Complex.* Chico, CA: AK Press, 2001.

Heitzeg, Nancy A. *The School-to-Prison Pipeline: Education, Discipline, and Racialized Double Standards.* Santa Barbara, CA: Praeger, 2016.

Hinton, Elizabeth. *From the War on Poverty to the War on Crime: The Making of Mass Incarceration in America.* Cambridge, MA: Harvard University Press, 2017.

Kilgore, James. *Understanding Mass Incarceration: A People's Guide to the Key Civil Rights Struggle of Our Time.* New York: The New Press, 2015.

Lordan, Christopher, and Robert Dellelo. *The Factory: A Journey Through the Prison Industrial Complex.* Scotts Valley, CA: CreateSpace, 2016.

Macías-Rojas, Patrisia. *From Deportation to Prison: The Politics of Immigration Enforcement in Post-Civil Rights America.* New York: NYU Press, 2016.

Parenti, Christian. *Lockdown America, Police and Prisons in the Age of Crisis.* Brooklyn, NY: Verso, 2008.

Peterson, James Braxton. *Prison Industrial Complex for Beginners.* Hanover, NH: Steerforth Press, 2016.

Pfaff, John. *Locked In: The True Causes of Mass Incarceration—and How to Achieve Real Reform.* New York: Basic Books, 2017.

Scheffler, Judith A. *Wall Tappings: Women's Prison Writings, 200 A.D. to the Present.* New York: The Feminist Press at CUNY, 2002.

Sered, Danielle. *Until We Reckon: Violence, Mass Incarceration, and a Road to Repair.* New York: The New Press, 2019.

Ward, Jesmyn. *Sing, Unburied, Sing: A Novel.* New York: Scribner, 2018.

Wehr, Kevin. *Beyond the Prison Industrial Complex: Crime and Incarceration in the 21st Century.* Abingdon-on-Thames, England: Routledge, 2013.

Index

O

Obama, Barack, 30, 106, 111–112, 114–115, 122, 154, 155, 156, 160

opioid epidemic, 55–57

P

Pearl, Betsy, 52–60

people of color and prison, 15, 23–24, 32–37, 51, 54, 59, 74, 77, 78, 82, 87, 88–94, 95, 99, 101–104, 120, 133, 135–136, 141, 144–145, 150–151

Pfaff, John, 61–65

Phelps, Michelle S., 121–126

poverty and prison, 23–24, 34–35, 82, 88–94, 133–134

prison abolition movement, 120, 140–152

prison industrial complex

defined, 14, 17, 19

economic and social implications, 82

future of, 120

as modern-day slavery, 35–37

overview, 18–24

as self-perpetuating system, 20–21, 36–37

what caused/started it, 20–21, 51

who benefits from, 21–23, 25–31, 36–37, 64, 105–117, 123, 147, 154, 155, 158–159

Prison Industry Enhancement Certification Program (PIECP), 39–44

prison labor, 14, 15, 28–29, 36, 82, 141, 146

argument for it being beneficial, 38–44

prison reform, 15, 35, 45, 65–66, 126, 127–131, 152

privatization of prisons, issue of, 45–48, 51, 64–65, 68–69, 146–147

R

Reagan, Ronald, 20, 30, 62

recidivism, 36, 39, 41–42, 48, 58, 130–131, 151

Red Sky in the Sun, 140–152

rehabiliation, 14, 18, 21, 22, 42–43, 48, 56, 62, 120, 140, 147, 148, 149, 151

Republican Party, 27, 78, 113, 121, 122, 124–126, 161

retribution vs. rehabilitation, idea of, 14–15, 148–149

Riley, Rick, 28–29

Robertson, Joe, 68, 71–72

S

Sanders, Bernie, 48, 78

Schlosser, Eric, 14, 82

school-to-prison pipeline, 82, 95–104, 132–139

defined, 96

sentencing laws, harsh, 18, 20, 51, 53, 62, 64, 76, 96

Sessions, Jeff, 115, 122, 126, 155